THANKS AND ACKNOWLEDGEMENTS

I would like to thank all the women who have contributed to and inspired this book.

So I'll begin with a massive thank you to my mother Maddie and my big sister Corinna, who taught me so much when I was young.

Thank you to all the kick-ass women who have been my clients, friends, partners, colleagues and teachers. Thank you for sharing your perspectives, for pointing out my dumb assumptions, for showing me how bad it can be for women in our culture, and for working with me to find better ways to find balance and fairness.

I'd like to thank all those women who have, across the centuries, fought for justice and fairness in society: writing inspiring books, challenging prevailing beliefs and educating generations of feminists.

And thank you to all the men I've known who have taught me how to be a good man: to know when to stand up and be heard, and when to shut up and listen.

Red Flags

10 TYPES OF TOXIC MEN
HOW TO AVOID DATING THEM
HOW TO AVOID BEING ONE

Alexander Butler

CONTENTS

INTRODUCTION

A book about hope

Welcome to this book about relationships. We're going to be talking about forming deep connections, understanding one another, building great relationships...and some of the biggest things that get in the way. There's also going to be a big focus on staying safe and aware when you're looking for love.

When a romantic relationship really works, when two people come together in love and find ways to communicate effectively, it's the most wonderful thing in the world. It's difficult, it challenges us like nothing else will, but wow it's rewarding. It can bring us happiness, fulfilment, companionship, support of all kinds, and it brings warmth and richness to everything else in our lives. It tends to boost our wellbeing, our confidence and our self-esteem. That's why we persist, even when we're hurt or rejected or messed around. That's why we keep putting ourselves out there.

I am a Master Life Coach, philosopher and author based in the UK. Every day, I meet clients and we work hard to solve problems and challenges. I've been hired by people who want to save their marriages, by people who want to end their relationships with grace, by people who don't know whether to stay or to go, by people who have invested decades into their relationships and who don't want to let go even though it's become toxic as hell, by people who've learned to recognise their own toxic patterns and who want to ensure that their half of the relationship is honest, and healthy and fair. I've had that rare perspective of being welcomed into someone's life completely. My clients get to be completely vulnerable and open with me. So I've been lucky enough to learn from so many people about so many kinds of relationships.

I'm also somebody who's experienced amazing, joyful relationships that made me laugh and dance and feel happy and grateful, and I've had those relationships that messed me up, let me down or broke my heart. I've been shaken and hurt. So I write this both as an expert on the human condition, and as someone who's been there and done that.

The fundamentals of relationship

What is a relationship?

Well, that's obvious, right? It's two people who've decided they're 'together'?

Except it isn't obvious. Not at all. Everyone has their own idea about what a relationship is meant to be, and if we're not conscious of all our assumptions and all the emotional needs we're bringing along, and if we don't recognise the things that influence the way we treat our partner, we're at risk of getting into repeating patterns.

Unconscious relationships are, usually, doomed relationships. Even if they last, through stubbornness or the fear of being alone, they won't be happy relationships.

In the beginning, it's usually simple. You meet someone, there's a spark, and your hormones take over. Some hormones are about sex, others are about bonding. That initial overwhelming, awe-inspiring, intoxicating feeling of being 'in love'? That's hormones. Be sure to enjoy them! But they will fade. They exist in mammals to make sure we stick around long enough to have babies. When your body realises that babies aren't happening, the hormone balance will shift. From then on, it's more complicated.

In a conscious relationship, we begin to have conversations about what we really want. Are we looking for something long-term here? Do we want to live together eventually? Are we talking about children? Is the ideal holiday all about lying on a beach, or do we want to go paragliding and trekking through the mountains together? Do we want to heal our relationship patterns? Can we be completely honest and 'own our stuff' in this relationship?

Sooner or later, I end up talking to most of my clients about love and relating, so I've had to come up with a way of explaining what a relationship is. Here's what I tend to say...

You bring stuff to every relationship: your needs, desires, fears and expectations. You have a lifetime of experiences. You have happy memories of how a relationship can be. You have memories of hurt, betrayal, disappointment or rejection in your adult life, which you'd love to avoid in the future. You have early-life conditioning: the way your parents, siblings and teachers treated you, and the ways in which those lessons shaped your feelings around love, vulnerability and communication. You've got wounds and emotional scars. You do things sometimes that you don't understand, or say things you don't really mean.

You feel proud about some things: your achievements, your choices, your appearance or hard-won abilities. You've got a certain level of skill in expressing your feelings and needs to other people, and in empathising with their feelings and needs. You are a complex melting pot of ideas, feelings, beliefs, fears, needs, longings and hopes, some of which you're conscious of, while others lurk in your unconscious mind.

And then, you meet someone else equally complex. They have all their stuff. They have history, and early life conditioning, and wounds, and happy memories, and fears. They have things they're avoiding and things they're seeking. They, like you, have a certain amount of

*conscious knowledge of themselves, and loads of unknowns that baffle
even themselves.*

*The two of you come together and say: I'm this complex mess, you're
that complex mess. Can our complexities and backgrounds play well
together? Can we make this work?*

"

Nobody comes to a relationship as a simple person. The more you
know yourself, the more you can take responsibility for all the
complexity you bring. The more your partner knows themselves,
the more they can do the same.

This is one of the big reasons that everyone should engage in
personal development work.

This book is not anti-men

Everyone has personal 'stuff'. Perhaps your parents taught you
really bad life lessons. Perhaps you've been through hard things
that left their mark on you. Perhaps you've done some things you're
not proud of. When we go through difficult things in life, especially
when we're young and impressionable, we adapt ourselves, usually unconsciously. We might become more or less emotional, or
more or less likely to take risks, or we might shift our perceptions
or beliefs about things. This is really psychology 101: everyone is
unique because we've all been shaped by the lives we've lived. We

arrive in adulthood with various adaptations, some of them really smart, some of them the result of traumatic events that have led to some really dysfunctional adaptations.

This is true for everyone.

There are wounds and quirks and complexities inside you that are unique to you, but there are also loads of things that are general, society-wide problems. There are widespread beliefs that have no basis in evidence, or science or fact, but which we pass from generation to generation.

An example would be parents who don't believe in themselves, who teach their children that they shouldn't take risks. Risk-taking is essential for healthy self-esteem, and to live a rich and varied life. Those parents have repressed their children's potential, and it's only when those children grow up and 'do the work' to examine what's going on under the hood that they notice the limiting beliefs their parents have passed on to them.

In this book, I'll be talking a lot about problems. We're going to be looking at types of toxic men in the area of relationships. To be very clear: there is nothing inherently toxic about men. Men are just people. They will have their own personal 'stuff' that they picked up early in life, and they've experienced knocks and hurts as adults, just like most women have.

The problem, as I'll be unpacking in the next chapter, is not men. The problem is the enormous cultural baggage that most people in our culture are exposed to, and the things we're programmed to believe from birth. Women are expected to be many things, and so are men. Again, none of these beliefs are based in objective, scientific research. No smart people sat down, with all the relevant information to hand, and decided that we should teach boys and girls to behave like this. They're just beliefs that have been passed down without question.

The driving force behind human psychology (our feelings, beliefs, thoughts, habits, decision-making, etc) are our mental and emotional needs. Here's a simple diagram of Maslow's famous 'Hierarchy of Needs'. This is the stuff we're all chasing after, and trying to find in whatever ways we can...

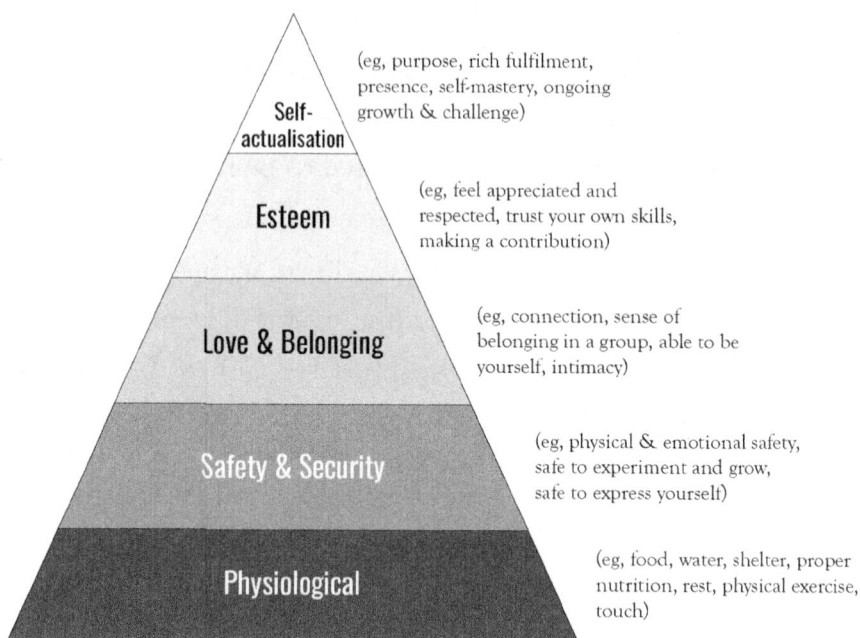

We grow up learning ways to find these things, and we learn new ways throughout life. When we have gaps, we feel like something is missing, or wrong, or we feel unhappy and unsatisfied. Speaking very simply: the more of these needs that are satisfied, the happier life becomes.

When we're young, people teach us ways of meeting these needs, mostly based on their own life experience. Some of these lessons are great, and effective, and smart. Some of them are counterproductive, or actually cause us harm, or leave us vulnerable in all sorts of ways.

I don't want to go too deep into this (I've written other books about finding lasting happiness) but the simple formula is:

1. We're born with a big set of intrinsic personal needs

2. Each of these needs exerts subtle (or sometimes really obvious) pressure on us until we find a way to fulfil it

3. A lot of our early life learning is being taught strategies to satisfy these needs. Our parents and teachers and mentors needed to solve the same problems, and they pass their solutions on to us

4. Some solutions are smart. Some solutions are harmful.

Men have the same needs that women have, they're searching for the same things. However, there is a cultural straight-jacket tied around almost every man, which shuts down his choices and leaves him trapped, struggling and (often) alone. Men are not the problem, any more than women are the problem. As we'll go on to explore, the straight-jacket is the problem. It's this cultural binding that can leave men erratic, volatile, dangerous or struggling to communicate effectively.

Women have personal psychological baggage, and they also have cultural programming that they need to work hard to shed. This book isn't intended to paint women as better than men, or free of their own programming and toxic behaviour.

However, in this book we're focused on toxic men, how they became that way, and what can be done about it. Each individual man has his personal issues that he can work on, and he is also part of a society-wide brainwashing programme.

Women, who were traditionally repressed and under-represented in society, have fought back. Women today have decades of feminist thought to draw on, which now pops up in all sorts of popular movies and TV shows, and women are usually more likely to engage in personal development work, ask for help, reflect on their motivations or go to therapy.

Men were the benefactors of that repression. They didn't create a movement to understand themselves, and men are much less likely to ask for help. Today, the ways in which personal issues and cultural programming show up in men is, sadly, quite predictable. As we'll explore, men's cultural brainwashing prepares them for a world that no longer exists, and this is the source of their problems. We end up with depressingly predictable patterns of behaviour, and in this book I've simply picked 10 common ways in which this programming and psychological pain show up in men.

Every man can heal. Every man can work on his personal psychological complexities and he can work on how much he believes the cultural programming he's received. So this book isn't meant to demonise anyone, to judge anyone as having failed, or to push a simplistic idea that men are evil, toxic or inherently broken.

This book is packed with advice about how that man can heal, and indeed how women might need to heal if they continue to find these men attractive.

This book has a purpose: to enable people to find lasting love in safe, fulfilling relationships by understanding one another. So I don't assume that either women or men are inherently better than their partner. I also don't have any sympathy for women or men who continue toxic behaviour throughout their lives: no amount of pain or programming is an excuse for bad or hurtful behaviour.

My question for men: what do you really want?

This book will be a deep dive into the psychology that traps so many men in beliefs, thoughts and feelings that hurt them and hurt the people around them.

For most women, the reasons for figuring out this stuff tend to be pretty obvious. They want fulfilling relationships, they want to be close to men who are mentally and emotionally well, they want to be able to trust their partners, and they don't want to be the victims of manipulation, abuse or violence.

Lurking within our culture are some collections of ideas and beliefs that deny the freedom and humanity of women. Under these beliefs, women are reduced to being accessories and chattels to men. When women are subjected to these beliefs (as long as they haven't internalised these beliefs themselves) they will immediately feel oppressed. So the motivation to be a feminist, as a woman, and fight for freedom and self-determination are pretty strong and obvious.

Men don't experience this oppression, or this denial of their humanity and identity, so the motives to solve this problem aren't as obvious. I will be exploring all the pain and hardship that men experience as a result of their programming. In part I'm doing this so women who read this book will deeply understand the psychology of the men in their lives. In part I'm writing this so men can find greater and stronger reasons to 'do the work'. Men don't have the motives of being ignored at work, or scared to go out at night on their own, or the fear of a violent partner. Men need other motives. In this book I'll be sharing a lot of those motives from a very self-serving perspective: if you don't want low self-esteem, or if you don't want to be lonely in your life, or if you want romantic relationships that feel fantastic, then do the work.

However, there is one really simple reason why men should care about personal development, about cultural programming and about feminism. Put simply, a deeply fulfilling life is simply not possible while these beliefs still exist within you.

Men, do you want these things?

- To be able to have emotionally rich, deeply connected relationships
- A fun and passionate sex life
- Your own unshakable inner strength and confidence
- For the women in your life to feel safe, empowered and free to choose whatever life will bring them the most freedom
- The ability to understand the things your partner tells you, especially when she's sharing her trouble and problems with you
- To know how to respond to her in a way that will bring you both closer, rather than both feeling frustrated or upset
- To know that your partner will stay with you into later life
- To feel mentally, emotionally and spiritually fulfilled

If you want those things (which, I would argue, are some of the cornerstones of a healthy, fulfilling adult life) then you will need to do the work.

- You need to examine the programming and beliefs you received in childhood
- You need to learn to feel and understand your feelings
- You will need to be sure you're free to communicate everything you feel with the people who matter most to you.

The stuff in this book, and the history of feminist thought, is about the flourishing of all people. Yes, there are bad actors within the feminist world who trip over into misandry or man-hating. That's not really feminism. Feminism is simply the idea that we're all people, we all deserve freedom, and we all need to connect deeply with other human beings. To achieve these things, I'd ask men to read the words in this book and consider what work you might need to do on yourself.

What will you get from this book?

I've written this book with both women and men in mind.

We're living through an odd time in history, a time that's been shaped by technology, by certain huge events and by the shared beliefs we all carry in our mind and in our hearts. The 20th century saw the rise of feminism and the rejection of traditional gender roles, and while most people now agree with the idea of equality, most of us still have dark corners of our thinking and feeling that promote inequality in our language, or our choices, or just in the way we see things. For example, men will tend to apply for jobs they're under-qualified for, whereas women will generally only apply for a job if they're sure they meet all the requirements. Where does that come from? What beliefs underpin those habits?

I'll be going into more detail about these beliefs in the next chapter because we can't navigate relationships unless we know what subtle influences are manipulating our thoughts.

However, so much traditional certainty is gone. Today, everyone has to find their own way in dating and relationships. Each person you meet will have their own unique views, feelings and opinions about the roles of men and women, and we tend to react very strongly when some of these fundamental beliefs are challenged. You will meet women who yearn for a very old-fashioned relationship where they can be a home-maker. You will meet people who reject the concept of gender. You will meet men who are striving to be self-aware and 'work on themselves', but who struggle to know what they're 'allowed' to say any more. Then there are always bad actors: women and men who are hostile towards one another and use terrible behaviour to attack, manipulate and abuse. It's chaos out there, and it's often chaos inside ourselves.

I hope this book can be an antidote for this chaos, for you.

The benefits for women

If you're a woman who likes to date men, this book is designed to help you avoid the most common types of toxic men. Men who will hurt you, abuse you, degrade your self-esteem or downgrade your life. Every relationship has the potential to break your heart, that's just the risk we take falling in love, but some men are particularly dangerous and this book is designed to help you spot them.

Beyond that, I've written this book so you understand why some men are like that, and also why you're attracted to them even though they're bad for you. So many women date a series of men who have the same negative traits, and they come to the conclusion that all men are like that, or they just get really frustrated with themselves that they keep falling for the same kind of men.

This book is designed to help you grow or heal beyond the desire to date toxic men.

The benefits for men

If you're a man reading this book then first of all, thank you! You're already one of the small number of men who are willing to seek help or get fresh perspectives. So many men find this impossible, and remain trapped in a single perspective their whole lives.

By reading this book, I hope you get a better understanding of what women go through when they're dating and in relationships with men, and why they talk so often about how awful men are. Men aren't awful. Men are just people. But there are a lot of men who treat women very badly.

If you're a man who's seeking to be a good, supportive, safe, trustworthy partner then it's a good idea to learn what the dating landscape is like for women. Learn what toxic traits pop up in other men. Notice it in your friends and call them out on it.

Later in this book there are 10 types of toxic men, and most men fall into one or more of these groups, at least a little bit. So this book is also about your healing and growth: what toxic stuff is still alive in you, and how do you fix it?

What do I mean by 'toxic'?

It's really common today, especially online, to put labels on people we don't understand, or diagnose them with disorders, or call them toxic. The word is thrown around a lot, so I want to be clear what I mean by toxic beliefs, or behaviour, or people.

Things that are *not* toxic include:

- Being annoying
- Having a different opinion
- Being emotional, such as being grumpy after a bad day or getting angry about something
- Making mistakes
- Wanting a better life
- Communicating clear boundaries or saying no

In my mind, being 'toxic' requires 3 things:

1. Doing things, saying things or believing things that cause harm to people. In particular, these things degrade someone's quality of life, their health, their wellbeing, their self-esteem and their potential. Being toxic means to be harmful to a healthy life.

2. These things continuing to happen over a long time. People can be hurtful sometimes, or thoughtless, or inconsiderate, or mean. Toxicity means that it keeps happening, day after day, year after year.

3. There is an obvious and easy way to be better, to do better, to treat people better. Usually this means unlocking more understanding, empathy and compassion.

So we're talking about psychological poisoning, just like a chemical would poison an environment. Somebody who does things, says things or believes things that are toxic is like a leaking barrel of chemicals, spoiling and degrading the lives of the people around them.

We'll be exploring how some men get like this and what can be done about it.

The 10 types of toxic men

Later in this book I'll be exploring 10 types of toxic men. For each type I'll explain:

- What makes them unique and dangerous
- What psychology is driving these men
- What makes them attractive to women
- What might heal this type of man

As a coach, everything I do is supposed to be effective and practical, so I've created these 10 groups of toxic men to give women a way to identify what's going on in the men they meet, and for men it's a way to identify where they, personally, need to focus their growth. It's also important that men challenge toxic behaviour in other men, so the types are there to support men's efforts in doing this.

A lot of men fall into several types. It would be normal to find a man who's an overt Misogynist (Type 1), who's also a Stone (Type 4) and a Pornosexual (Type 6).

The point of the system is for women to be safer, more aware and better able to navigate their relationships, and for men to identify the toxic traits that lurk within them and to know what to do about them.

About me

Today I am an internationally renowned Master Life Coach and a philosopher. I work with coaching clients every day to deeply explore the challenges they're facing and make meaningful, effective plans to solve them. This is intense, profound, life-changing work and my clients grow enormously as people, confronting the very deepest mental and emotional blocks and learning entirely new ways to live. I hear words like "I've never felt like this before" pretty regularly. Alongside coaching, I facilitate groups, write books and publish videos on YouTube.

I have been doing this for over 15 years now, and I didn't let myself start work with actual clients until I was sure I knew what I was doing. A Life Coaching qualification wasn't anywhere near enough for me. By the time I was first paid as a coach, I had a degree in philosophy and I'd read extensively about all sorts of similar subjects: indigenous practices and beliefs; anthropology; neuroscience; the theory of how people change. I had run my own businesses, had a wide range of jobs and side-hustles, I'd learned from every expert I was able to meet and I'd engaged in a wide range of spiritual traditions. This felt like a solid foundation to begin helping people navigate their own lives, and I continue to try to learn new things every day. Some of my ongoing learning is from active study, but much of it comes from my clients. I've now got over 15 years of insights into all sorts of industries, organisations, styles of parenting, healing journeys and types of relationships.

But so much of my expertise, and so much of my motivation in writing this book, began in my childhood.

I was raised mostly by women, and those women were actively involved in their own healing. Throughout my childhood my mother was studying psychology, and I helped her revise for her exams. It was normal at the dinner table for us to be talking about emotions, mental habits, personal development, boundaries and theories from Abraham Maslow or Carl Rogers. When I brought my first serious girlfriend home to meet my family, she took me aside and said "you guys talk about your feelings all the time!".

My parents divorced when I was 6, and my dad took a big leap and launched his own business in the oil industry in Aberdeen, Scotland, while I was living in rural Cornwall in the South West of England. He wanted to be close to me, so he bought a house nearby just so I could live with him for one week in 4. Every school holiday he'd fly me up to Scotland to see him. He worked very hard and he paid for the expensive public school I attended.

He was, and is, a pretty traditional guy. You never really know what he's thinking or feeling. He lives in a closed-off world. He grew up in poverty and worked his way to the top of everything he did. I was always very proud of my dad, he has some truly extraordinary achievements in his life and even in later life he continues to excel…but I never really understood him and he felt pretty distant to me.

Of course, throughout my childhood my mum and big sister were dating, or telling me about encounters with men. I began to learn, at a young age, that there are a lot of bad men out there who treat women very badly. This has carried on into my coaching work. I've had very few female clients who didn't tell me about emotionally distant partners, or men who spoke over them in meetings at work, or men who actively abused them. At the same time, most men I worked with have had big gaps in their skills around understanding and managing themselves - especially their emotions and beliefs.

I was trained as a coach at Embercombe in Devon which was, at the time, a world-leading centre for leadership and personal development. There, I worked alongside fierce feminists who opened my eyes to the deeper theory of 'patriarchy' and the ways that men and women are brainwashed to conform to outdated roles that stop them being their true selves. Even in a modern, much more emancipated world, the roots still run deep.

So finally, after years of speaking with women about all these awful, or violent, or disappointing, or emotionally straightjacketed men, I decided to start creating material. My two videos on YouTube about patriarchy and toxic masculinity are popular (with a big spike in views after the release of the Barbie movie in 2023) and I've been interviewed by researchers about my knowledge and experience of patriarchy in a personal development and healing context.

I am not a perfect man. I make mistakes, and sometimes I say things, do things or find myself believing things that don't sit well with me. I have been challenged by women and men across my lifetime to do better and be better, and I'm deeply grateful to the people who helped me realise my bad patterns. Writing this book, I can still see so much in me that needs work. But I am committed to that work.

Why did I write this book?

The real motivation behind this book came out of my coaching work. Hours and hours listening to women talk about their dating experiences or the way their partners treat them. Hours of speaking to men about things they've inherited from their fathers about their expectations or beliefs about women...

- Men who can't talk about their feelings
- Men who randomly explode in anger or violence
- Men with no dreams, goals or aspirations who sabotage their partners' dreams just to avoid looking at their own lack of self-belief
- Men who expect sex to feel and look like porn
- Men who intentionally use, manipulate, or exploit women

- Men who refuse to look at their emotional or traumatic issues, which in turn introduces things into the relationship like addiction, financial problems, violence, constant fights, prevailing misery, or a feeling 'walking on eggshells'

- Men who embarrass or humiliate women at work to keep their own power, or just for fun

- Men who hate their mothers, and take out their resentment on the women they meet

- Men who seduce women, promising them the world, just to get an ego boost or a quick shag

- Men who share women's naked selfies with their mates

- Men who still believe in 'stupid women', 'crazy emotional bitches' or tropes about women being terrible drivers (sorry guys but, statistically speaking, women are much, much better drivers than men)

These stories are so common, and I hear them almost constantly. It's rare for me to go more than a few days without hearing a story like this from a woman. Meanwhile, I hardly ever hear stories about mean or hurtful women.

So whatever's going on in men is really common, and what's really driven me to write this book is the knowledge that *it doesn't need to be like this*. I bury my head in my hands when I hear about another man who behaves terribly towards women. I'm embarrassed to be grouped in with men like that. I'm frustrated that men are still behaving so badly towards women. I'm astonished that it's still normal, that so many men still haven't sorted themselves out.

Most of all, I'm furious that so many vibrant, interesting, kick-ass women have been hurt so badly, sometimes traumatised, often physically abused, and that this has often altered the trajectory of their lives. Women who have learned not to trust anyone any more, or women who have adapted to accept bad behaviour in order to find love, or women whose careers have been sabotaged by misogynists at work.

As a society, we should be better than this.

I want to say again, there's nothing inherently wrong with men. Men aren't born bad. What's happened is that cultural programming has seeped into the beliefs, perspectives and behaviour of most people (women and men), and this programming encourages men to see women as less important, less valuable and less human than men. I believe that most men are badly wounded and in need of healing, therapy and a supportive community. At the same time, the same programming that lets them see women as objects or as playthings, tells them that asking for help or engaging in healing is a personal failure.

In this book, I'll explore and unpack this programming.

A note to LGTBQ+ readers, or those in poly relationships

I have clients from every possible background. So long as the fundamentals of respect, care and healthy boundary-setting are there, I respect anyone's way of finding love and belonging.

However, this book is aimed at addressing the nature of patriarchal beliefs, and how they poison relationships between men and women. Perhaps when I feel I understand enough I'll write books for other forms of relationships…but there are probably a lot of authors out there who are better qualified to write them.

PART ONE: THE PROBLEM

Some key terms

My coaching clients often want to explore the themes of relationships, sex and identity during our sessions. It often comes up organically during conversations, or sometimes they've hired me because they want to work on their marriage, or because they want help finding a relationship, or sometimes because they want to end a relationship in a caring, healthy, graceful way. So I hear a lot about a lot of different kinds of relationships, from different perspectives, and at different stages.

In this chapter I'm just going to talk about a few key terms and phrases that I'll be using throughout this book. Language has a huge effect on the way we think and feel about things, and I want to be sure we're on the same page.

I'll be diving into some theory to begin with. Some of it might seem obvious to you, especially if you've had to live with sexism or discrimination. I'm going to go through how people inherit their core beliefs, how cultures work, and why our current culture has created this perfect storm of circumstances where toxic masculinity is allowed to thrive.

I'll try to cover it all quickly, but if you notice phrases or ideas that interest you, please take the time to research them more fully. There's nothing revolutionary or unusual in the theory I'm about to cover, and writers and educators around the world have covered all the core ideas in much more detail.

Early life programming

Psychologists do a lot of research on children. Since my mum was a psychologist, I myself was part of studies at the University of Plymouth when I was a toddler (I don't remember what happened, it probably involved brightly coloured bricks). It's given us a fairly good idea of what happens during early brain development, the different stages we go through and how children learn. Big discoveries are still being made, and theories change, but a lot is known and understood.

The first few years of somebody's life is a time of rapid brain development, when many of our core beliefs about the world are laid down, along with all sorts of other things that will define the rest of our lives. When we're young, and probably only learning from a few primary caregivers (usually our parents, maybe siblings or grandparents), we are constantly learning. We learn how to move and control our bodies, we learn how to communicate our basic needs and we slowly learn to handle complex situations. We're sponges at this age, taking on information of all kinds. We don't have the ability to compare what we're learning to what other children are learning until much later, so we have no way of knowing what's healthy and true, from what is simply our parents' dysfunction, neurosis or unhealthy beliefs.

Often, later in life, we begin to notice how weird our family is. Perhaps we go to college in another town and people laugh at something we do. We begin to realise that, in the wider world, people think differently. This is one of the main reasons why travel is so good for us: we get a fresh perspective on everything, and we get a chance to re-examine our core beliefs about the world.

Until this re-examining happens, we believe what we're taught. So, people who grow up in different kinds of homes will become different kinds of people. Some of our character will be the result of our genes, but the things that happen to us in early life certainly have a massive impact on the things we believe, the ways we feel and the choices we make.

Other layers are added later in life, especially at school where it becomes so important to fit in and conform. For teenagers, the priority tends to be connecting and being accepted, so we learn a lot of our social habits during this time.

Nobody is racist, or sexist, or misogynist, or toxic, or abusive when we're born. We have to be programmed to become those things. Parents and other carers will teach us what they believe about the world, and if they happen to have toxic or hostile beliefs, we will absorb them alongside the other lessons about life.

This is early-life programming, and it's one of the key things we all need to understand about ourselves. Therapy tends to examine and explore the beliefs that we absorbed as children, but didn't realise that we did. Exposure to other perspectives, other beliefs or other backgrounds also helps us challenge all the things we think are true.

From my perspective, there are few things in life that are as important as this. You should understand the ground you stand on, to be sure that your life is built on strong foundations.

Do you know what beliefs you were taught as a child?

Cultural Programming

We all have core memories from childhood. Certain places we played, or the house we grew up in. If I asked you what it was like when you had your evening meals as a kid, you could probably tell me all about it. Did you sit together as a family? Did you watch TV? Did people sit in particular places? Was it just you and your mum? Did it feel like a happy time or a tense time? What kind of food did you eat?

We grow up in little bubbles, disconnected from the wider world. Sure, you go out into the world sometimes when you're young, but there are usually comfort zones that we live in for most of the time. The home, a few local spots and later, school.

What we don't notice is that this whole scene is bathed in the beliefs of our culture. We can't see it until much later, because we learn that it's normal, and we can't see things that are normal.

Culture is the shared beliefs that we all carry, because they're taught to us from day 1 by our parents, through our education, by books and TV, by social media. It's not usually taught explicitly, it's usually implied. It's the deeper beliefs behind everything, it's all the things that nobody says, but the things we say wouldn't make sense if we didn't all believe these things. We all unconsciously absorb these beliefs and don't question them, so it's like a mass agreement we've all made with each other about the way the world is. But they are beliefs, they're not facts.

Here are some examples of cultural beliefs that different people grow up with:

- God exists and our religion is right
- Women wear skirts and men wear trousers
- A person should always succeed on their own
- Certain genders, religions or races are better than others
- Rich people are better human beings than poor people
- Some lifestyles or careers are meant for women, some are meant for men
- The importance of personal property and privacy
- We expect the future to be better than the past
- You can trust these newspapers, you can't trust those ones
- Women should be thin
- Men should be muscular
- We should respect our elders
- We should eat 3 meals a day

- Some accents tell you that those people are smart

- These clothes are fashionable, those clothes aren't

- Scepticism towards government or experts OR reverence of government or experts

- It's good to show off your wealth and success OR it's shameful/vulgar to show off your wealth

- Our country is better than their country

Each culture has its own answers to some of the great questions: what really matters? What does it mean to be a woman or to be a man? What is success and what is failure? What things should we desire and feel proud of achieving, and what should we feel shame about? How do we reward one another for that kind of success? How do we handle family life, spiritual beliefs, illness and death, or relationships? All of this stuff has strong cultural beliefs behind it. You'll find different answers to these questions in different cultures around the world, and sometimes between counties, regions or states.

Culture, then, is always in the background. It's implied by lots of things we say to each other, and it's a way to reassure ourselves that we're safe, that we belong. Belonging is an intrinsic human need and, as social animals, we will usually want to fit in with a group. Culture is the assumptions and broad beliefs of a group, and it can be difficult to spot your own cultural programming.

Again, it's important that we each examine how we've been programmed by our culture. Cultural programming isn't true, it's just a set of beliefs that we happen to participate in. They can make us unhappy, they can restrict our freedom, they can compel us to hurt other people, all without us noticing.

Esteem and Shame

Cultures, then, are big webs of beliefs that tell us all who we should be.

Shame is a very strong emotion, which is used by cultures to keep people from doing the wrong things. Certain behaviour, or words, or choices, or lifestyles would be seen as shameful.

Shame is a very uncomfortable feeling. If we do something shameful, we feel a pressure to conform, to change what we're doing to rid ourselves of this horrible feeling of shame. Many families are dominated by shame: if we say the wrong words, or do unusual things, or date the wrong people, we'll get told off, or shamed in some way. For example, I always think about my father's response every time he sees my tattoos. They're shameful to him, and he has to say something to tell me that I should feel ashamed.

Shame is thrown around all the time. Once you learn its language and all the expectations that everyone is putting on each other, you'll see shame flowing from one person to another, all the time. If you're interested to know more, I suggest you look into the work of Brene Brown. The videos of her TED talks, for instance, are brilliant.

At its heart, this is what shame is saying to us all the time: *if people saw me as I really am, people would reject me and nobody would ever really love me.*

We can spend our lives pretending to be people we're not, because we fear abandonment or rejection, and our childhoods are usually an education in the list of things that would cause people to reject or abandon us. An awful lot of people spend their whole lives afraid to be their authentic selves, and instead wear masks and pretend to be things they're not, just at the hope of fitting in and being loved.

Shame is a big part of the reason why so many men seem so broken and so toxic.

Esteem, meanwhile, is the opposite of shame. It's not a word we use a lot, except when we talk about 'self-esteem'. Esteem is what we earn when we do 'the right things'.

Traditionally, there was a universal list of things that earn esteem, but these days it's quite a personal thing. We unconsciously rank people in our heads, based on the things we think are most important in life. Perhaps rich people are better than poor people. Perhaps people who wear certain brands are better, or maybe it's people who drive certain cars. Certain accents can be seen as better than others. Certain careers.

You, like everyone, will have a list of things that are worthy of esteem to you, and the more of those you have yourself, the more self-esteem you have. If you believe that the best things in the world are money, love and a strong family life, you'll judge your own success and esteem based on these standards.

So without noticing, we're all navigating a complex dance of beliefs and feelings. We're all seeking simple things: things like security, connection, belonging, clear identity and purpose...but we seek these things through the lens of our culture. We were taught in our early lives what is good and what is shameful, and then school and our first jobs teach us a clear list of what qualities are best in ourselves and in the people around us. Certain choices will never occur to us, because they would carry so much shame if we did them. We spend our whole lives chasing things that might not even make us happy, because we grew up with some beliefs around what's best in life.

Some examples of this theory in action:

- We stay in miserable careers our whole lives because we were taught that the most important things in life are security and safety. We prioritise this over seeking deeper fulfilment.

- We stay in loveless marriages because we feel unbearable shame at the idea of divorce.

- We blow loads of money on luxury things, and take great comfort from them. Things like cars, or handbags, or branded clothes. Only later in life do we realise that these things, ultimately, feel hollow.

- We bounce between relationships because our partners never live up to our unconscious expectations (expectations we inherited from our parents).

Patriarchy (the true enemy)

If you look up the definition of Patriarchy, you'll read that it's a social system where wealth, property and titles can only be inherited by the male heirs of a family. For a great deal of European history, only men could legally inherit wealth when somebody passed away, and this was seen as completely normal and proper. That tells us a lot about the people who thought this was a normal thing to do. Why would you not pass your wealth on to women? Why would it seem weird to people that women could be independent, or be leaders, or hold wealth and political power? These people had clear beliefs about what men were meant to be like and what women were meant to be like, about the roles that genders were supposed to fulfil and about who should have the power.

So, patriarchy is also a set of beliefs about the roles of women and the roles of men. Feminism, which really took off in the 20th Century, is the international movement to dismantle patriarchy (or 'the patriarchy').

Patriarchy (not men) is the true target of feminism.

Patriarchy is taught to us, subtly, from our early lives. Almost all families still cling to some patriarchal beliefs. Very broadly, it's the idea that men have more value than women. In obvious and subtle ways, we can find examples all over our society of this belief:

- Men are paid more than women for equivalent work.

- Childcare (usually undertaken by women) is not seen as valuable work.

- Men talking over women during meetings at work, or men dismissing the ideas of women as less important than the ideas from men.

- How normal it is for men to watch pornography that turns women into sexual objects (often within an industry that causes tremendous physical and psychological harm to women).

- A woman being advised by her girlfriends to stay in an abusive relationship, because he's a great catch.

- Families where women are expected to conform to high standards where men can get away with anything and still be their parents' favourite.

- The idea that men are better drivers than women.

- In many places, it's still acceptable for men to stare at, objectify or wolf-whistle at women in public.

- Companies looking for the signature of 'the man of the house' rather than a woman's.

- Men dominating the world of politics.

- Women being attacked online by men, usually for their looks or for failing to make 'feminine' life choices.

All these things exist in our culture, and they all tell a story where men are better, or more valuable, than women. In many ways, it's still a man's world.

External and internal patriarchy

External patriarchy is when something happens in the world that promotes the rights of men and oppresses women. For example, when a man is hired for a job over a woman, even when she is better qualified and a better candidate, that's patriarchy at work.

However, if people grow up with patriarchal beliefs (as most of us did), we also carry these beliefs internally, and they influence us all the time. Why do women make loads of effort to look good for a date, but men can just turn up in jeans and a shirt? Why do women routinely diet so hard to keep themselves slim? Why do so many women feel a compulsion to keep their home immaculate, or clean everything when guests are coming to visit? Why do some women attack other women because they haven't had children?

Both women and men can have internalised patriarchy. This is the result of our early-life programming. It might come from our parents, our siblings, our school life, the movies and TV we watched, the books we read. If they're all telling us subtle things about how men are better than women, we'll begin to internalise patriarchal beliefs. This is why you find women making jokes about bad women drivers, or talking about how emotional and crazy women are, just as often as you hear men doing it. This is why women attack each other for not looking pretty enough or not wearing the right clothes.

We carry these patriarchal beliefs until we begin to question them and root them out. It's also, sadly, a lifelong project. You can spend ages identifying things you were taught as a child, only to find yourself saying something or feeling something that's motivated by beliefs that are hostile to your own wellbeing.

Everyone, to some degree, still carries some remnant of patriarchy within our thinking, feeling and belief. At the more extreme end, this explains women who campaign for all women to be stay-at-home mothers, or movements to ban abortions. But even the most evolved, self-aware person tends to still have echoes of patriarchal beliefs within them which pop up at the most unexpected time.

It's essential that we all try to be conscious of this, and not let these beliefs dominate our lives, our relationships and our choices.

The core beliefs of Patriarchy

Men gain respect and esteem for being:	It's shameful for men to be:
• Leaders • Decisive • Strong • Independent • Rich • Emotionless • Ready to use violence where necessary • Unchanging • Judgemental • Competitive	• Be emotionally expressive • Pursue art or expression • Ask for help • Seem vulnerable • Admit they're uncertain • Be silly or playful • Choose to be primary carers (stay at home parents)
Women gain respect and esteem for being:	**It's shameful for women to be:**
• Pleasing to men • Quiet, soft and elegant • Primary carers (stay at home parents) • Generally caring, especially towards men and boys • Deferential to men, being subservient • Fragile (to promote a man's feeling of strength) • Attractive and sexually available • Emotional	• Be loud • Express strength in any way • Pursue an independent life • Focus on her career • Be ruthless • Be more successful than a man • Fail to be attractive to men at all times • Show signs of ageing

Blindness towards patriarchy

This web of patriarchal beliefs hurt men almost as much as they hurt women. Men are manipulated to behave in ways that aren't really human. Studies have shown that boys aren't taught about emotions in the way girls are. Parents tend to use emotional language with girls ("how do you feel about that?", "oh you look happy", "what's made you sad?") whereas they don't use this language with boys. That's the patriarchy at work. These boys become men who can't identify, moderate or express their emotions, so they tend to be confused about how they feel, and they certainly can't express their feelings well. This leads to a great deal of loneliness, isolate, frustration and confusion in men, and I believe it accounts for the high suicide rates in men.

However, men are still being hired for good jobs and there are still some beliefs hanging around that help them to succeed. Patriarchy is still promoting men's success, as long as he conforms with the standards of patriarchy.

To the victims of any system, that system is obvious. When Martin Luther King gave his famous 'I Have a Dream' speech on the steps of the Lincoln Memorial, every black person in the crowd had experienced oppression at the hands of institutional racism. Similarly, every woman has stories of being attacked, ignored, sidelined, overlooked or abused simply for being a woman. It's obvious to any woman (who doesn't have strongly internalised patriarchy) that there are problems with the system.

So, women were (and often still are) repressed by the patriarchy. That's the point of it. Women have had to fight back against it. Early feminist writers were attacked, both intellectually and physically. Women have had to fight for the right to be heard - sometimes as part of a movement, but also on a personal level. Most women have strong memories of moments in their lives when they stood up to men and refused to be dominated.

Meanwhile, to the benefactors of an oppressive system, it's invisible, and simply feels right. Men are still, in terms of success in the world and most measures of esteem, the benefactors of patriarchy.

So it's easy for them to ignore the problem. Men who think of themselves as good will still allow patriarchy to work for them. They will still expect women to be pretty, obliging and available. They will still take advantage when their opinions are heard and a woman's is ignored. If their boss is a Misogynist, they might play along to get a promotion or a pay rise.

The price of patriarchy to women is their physical safety, their sense of self, their career prospects, their self-esteem, their right to a voice.

The price of patriarchy to men is more subtle. For men, the price is being able to form meaningful connections. The price is the expression of an authentic self. The price is being profoundly lonely for most of their life. The price is the expectation of a certain form of success, and the shame and judgement of others if he takes another route. The price is being forever stunted, both emotionally and spiritually.

But since these things aren't valued by patriarchy, he may never notice and if he does, he'll feel too ashamed to try to fix the things that are missing.

Othering

Othering is a thing our brains seem to want to do. We feel comfortable and cosy when we belong in a group, and it seems to be easier to belong to a group if we define ourselves by *not being like them*. It's also a lot easier to say things you *aren't* than to say things you *are*.

I trained to be a coach at a place called Embercombe, which at the time was a world-famous centre for personal development, leadership development and ecopsychology. At Embercombe, you might take part in a course or a workshop, and you'd do that in a big hall that was a converted aircraft hangar (the site used to be owned by a rich guy who used it as his own private airport). You would sleep in a yurt, and the yurts were arranged into two villages separated by a big hill so they couldn't see each other.

The founder of Embercombe, Mac, likes to tell a story about a group of corporate executives that came to Embercombe as part of their fast-track development. They all arrived on a big bus together, then they were separated into the two villages and told to go and dump their luggage in their yurts. Within half an hour, people in each village were talking about 'us' and 'them', meaning the people in our village and the people in the other village. 'We' are better than 'them'. 'They' are idiots. All that kind of thing. Without any kind of prompting or instruction, people in the East Village had decided they were better than people in the West Village, and vice versa.

This wasn't an isolated incident either. Each time a group came to Embercombe and set themselves up in one of the villages, they would quickly start talking about being better than the other village.

We easily form tribes, and we easily tell ourselves that our tribe is better, that their tribe is inferior, immoral, stupid or wrong. Political groups will have exaggerated and wild beliefs about their opposing political group; racial groups will tell one another things about other racial groups that make them into demons or weir-does; people in opposing companies or schools will tell themselves they're better or massively different to the other. It's not always negative: some groups can unconsciously believe that they are inferior to other groups.

'Othering' is the psychological component here. Human beings all share common genetic roots and we have far more in common than we have divisions, but there is this strong psychological temptation to make someone who is different to us into the 'other'. Othering means you're focusing on a huge gulf between you and them, it means the two of you have nothing in common, it means they are radically alien and divergent. We don't think of the other as being quite human in the same way we are human.

When someone walks down the street and sees a homeless person begging for change, it's easy to other them. When we see people protesting for something we don't agree with, it's easy to other them. When we see images of people from other countries doing things that we don't understand, it's easy to other them.

Once someone is 'othered', it's easy to dismiss them, ignore them, insult them, attack them or even kill them. In most war movies, the enemy has been 'othered', they've been portrayed as something totally alien, barely human, often totally evil. Moral distinctions are so much easier like this. When we've mentally categorised someone as other, we stop trying to understand them, or empathise with them, or form connections with them.

When othering happens between genders, we have a real problem. Men will other women by telling themselves, and talking to other men, about how crazy women are, or how much they nag, or how they love shopping more than anything else in the world. They roll their eyes at these weird, stupid, ridiculous creatures. They assume that women will only ever want certain stereotypical things, like children, or being a good wife, or a spa day, or being pampered by a rich man. Male policy makers will write laws that they believe are totally moral because they have othered women and only have the most superficial understanding of who they are and what they want.

Women, of course, also other men and come to believe that men are a totally alien species too. They tell themselves or each other that men are insensitive philistines, or exploiters, or big children. They might abandon the idea of expecting a lot from men because men are other, they can't understand women and there's no point in trying to communicate with them.

The antidote: Conscious living and conscious relationships

We are, as a species and as a culture, hugely limited by our personal and cultural programming, by our unchallenged beliefs and by our unconscious prejudices. There are things about our brains that we need to constantly challenge in order to make progress in our lives, and it's important that we are always willing to challenge ourselves and to be challenged by others. That's a cornerstone of personal growth and development.

For example, within personal development it's widely understood that there's a conflict between being happy and being comfortable. A part of our brains always wants us to be comfortable, even if that comfort is actually making us miserable. This part of us is always telling us that we should stay where we understand things, where we feel reassured, where things don't change. This is the comfort zone. But we all know that a life that never takes us outside our comfort zone leads to emotional and psychological problems, and it stops us learning and growing into stronger, happier people. We must challenge ourselves and risk being uncomfortable, regularly. But the risk-averse part of us will always tell us it's a bad idea. Just stay comfortable, stay safe, stay boring.

Conscious living is the antidote to so many problems. Conscious living means trying to be mentally and emotionally present in each moment. To live life in every breath. To be aware of ourselves and our surroundings. Beyond that, it means questioning things. Why do we do things that way? Is there a better way to do things? Is there information out there that can help us? It means exposing ourselves to things that feel alien and weird and different, because that experience of contrast allows us to notice things in ourselves that we haven't questioned before.

People who live this way succeed more, go further, build better relationships, parent their children better, and feel happier than people who live in unconscious loops.

Very few people are raised to live like this, and it takes effort to learn to do it. This is the core of my coaching work, and if you're interested in exploring this idea, please look for my trilogy of books called The Arete Trilogy, which is really focused on this idea of

Conscious Living: what is it, what holds us back, how do we find it and how do we stay there?

The psychology of wounded men

We all, then, grow up with certain programming. Some of it is obvious and conscious: there are things that we were taught when we were growing up that we still completely agree with, and we're conscious of that, and if somebody asked us to explain it, we'd be happy and able to do so. A great deal of our programming, though, is completely unrealised, unconscious and we don't notice when it guides our choices. That's normal, that's the human condition for most people.

Almost all men and women grew up in a patriarchal culture, to a greater or lesser extent. Almost all women and men have internalised patriarchy that subtly influences the things they think, feel and believe. Again, for some people this is a conscious thing that they're working on. These people might find themselves doing bad things and catch themselves, kick themselves and realise they've fallen for the old trap again. Other people don't notice when patriarchy is sneaking around in their minds. Women don't ask a guy out because something in their heads is telling them that he should make the first move. Men buy their partners a new vacuum cleaner as a gift because they think a woman's place is to stay home and clean.

Patriarchy puts women in physical and psychological danger, every day. Most women have stories about sexual violence, or men who got hostile when she said or did the wrong thing, or feeling afraid to go out at night. The effects of patriarchy on women are, often, really obvious.

Patriarchy also hurts men, every day. It constrains them, isolates them, causes them shame and self loathing. It accounts for the high rates of mental health issues and suicide in men.

How men get wounded

I'm trying to write this book with male and female readers in mind, but here I'm going to enter the complicated and confusing world of modern men's psychology.

There was a time when things were easier for men. Before feminism, before pluralism and political correctness and cultural integration. Things were simple then. Men knew what was expected of them, and the world had simple routes they could take to success, love, security and belonging. Different men will be thinking of different times as they read this, but most men know that there was a time that was very different from the world today.

For a lot of men, this might be something like the 1950s, when men were real men and women were real women and the world made sense. Of course this was a terrible time if you were a minority or a woman or if you were poor or if you were emotionally sensitive or if you were neurodivergent or if your marriage fell apart or if you didn't agree with the local pastor. The price of simplicity is always conformity.

Men continue to be just humans, looking to meet their core needs by whatever strategies they know and trust. However, the world is so much more complicated now, with different expectations and influences that directly conflict with one another.

It has become very, very difficult for a man to meet his intrinsic psychological needs without also feeling a sense of shame or failure.

Men are still expected to be independent, a lone wolf, a self-made man, strong in body and in mind, sexually virile, steadfast, wealthy, a provider for his family. Every man knows that he should be these things, and to some extent, every man feels a sense of shame and failure if he isn't these things. Since these standards aren't well defined any more, many men simply always feel like they're failing or, conversely, constantly congratulate themselves as doing incredibly well when actually their lives are a mess.

So, men are still judging themselves by old standards.

At the same time, a man knows that a lot of this is old-fashioned and unwelcome in the modern world. If he's self-aware, he knows that these old expectations don't lead to good places, he won't get the love and security and esteem that he craves if he just follows the old path. He will know that, along with the old standards, he's also supposed to be sensitive and communicative and caring. He's supposed to know how to listen, he's supposed to be patient, he's supposed to know how to show love and affection in ways women will appreciate. He's supposed to be all sorts of things that his unconscious patriarchal programming is telling him he shouldn't be.

It's not as simple as two conflicting narratives though. There are plenty of women out there who have just given up on men, so a man will meet women who are actively hostile towards him for no other reason than he's a man. He will receive messages every day offering him solutions to the things he feels he's lacking: buy these products, vote for these politicians, join these groups, listen to these social commentators. Each of these peddlers will have simplistic and ineffective answers for him, and each will add another layer of confusion to his life.

Patriarchy teaches a man to be independent and never ask for help, so many men will never get clarity on who they are, what they need and what solutions really work for them. They will either cling to the answers they learned in early life, or they will vacillate between answers people have sold them since.

So modern men are trapped between worlds. There will always be strong voices on all sides. His employer will discipline him if he's aggressive or sexual with women at work, but some celebrities and media personalities will tell him he should be a tyrant, a monster, he should grab women by the pussy and he should take what he wants from life. Like a 'real man'.

The human mind and spirit can only take so much shaming and lack of identity before it begins to break down. We evolved to be social animals who ensure our safety by knowing that we belong in a group. When we're exposed to impossible standards for too long, it begins to affect our mental health. In the language of psychology, men become wounded by this ongoing stress and lack of clarity. They want simple things, like all human beings do. They want to feel good about themselves, to have self-esteem and the esteem of people in their lives. They want to know where they belong. They want to feel purpose and meaning. They want to know they're doing well. But they can never truly reach these things, because one side or other of their identity is telling them they are failing.

The world today is full of wounded, confused, emotionally volatile men who feel terrible.

What are the core effects of this wounding?

EMOTIONAL INCOMPETENCE AND INFANTILISATION

Boys aren't taught how to understand or express their emotions in the same way girls are, and patriarchal programming tells a man that he should neither feel or express most emotions. Managing and expressing emotions is a skill and like any skill, it requires constant practice to master and maintain. Men are prevented from developing or maintaining these skills, so they tend to end up more emotionally incompetent or infantile than women. Many women have come to believe that all men are basically just big children. They come to believe that men are simply incapable of any meaningful emotional connection. There's no evidence that men have a smaller emotional range than women: it's simply that their skills have atrophied, or were never developed in the first place.

LONELINESS AND ISOLATION

Patriarchy tells a man that he should walk alone, that he should always know what he's doing, and that it's shameful to ask for help. You'll see campaigns on social media that encourage men to talk to each other more openly, or to talk about their problems, because most men will simply hold all their emotions, worries and problems inside until they burst.

Men are also often confused about how to approach women now. One side of his personality is telling him to be bold, to take risks, to say provocative things to excite and attract a woman, but experience has often taught him that many women don't want this any more. Some do, some don't. Some women want an emotionally sensitive man, some women find men like that repulsive. Some women know they *should* want a sensitive man, but they can only get turned on by a 'traditional' man. Right now, a growing number of women are very vocal about just hating all men. Dating has become very complex.

This all means that a lot of men are just very isolated and lonely. They don't know how to talk to their male friends, and they know that a lot of their male friends would mock them for being unmanly, while many men today struggle to know how to approach women.

SHAMING

Many men live with shame every day, whether or not they acknowledge it. The same can be said for women, but men's shame is less discussed. Men carry multiple voices in their heads, telling them conflicting stories about esteem and shame, and they know that they are probably failing on some front.

Shame feels like a weight, like a sense of personal failure, like there's something inherently wrong with you. It undermines self-esteem and confidence and it manipulates men's choices.

VULNERABILITY TO MANIPULATION

A man who was taught patriarchal values at home or at school will often spend most of their lives struggling with things like shame, self-esteem, belonging, intimacy and mental resilience. He is at the centre of a web of competing forces, telling him who he should be and how to achieve the things he longs for. Even the most self-aware and liberated man will occasionally fall victim to these forces, and men who haven't done the work to discover their unconscious needs leave themselves wide open to manipulation.

Men will choose careers that don't suit them, or buy products they don't need, or engage in hobbies they only vaguely enjoy, to try to tick the boxes and feel like a successful person. It's pretty easy to manipulate them to buy products, or vote for certain people, or join organisations. Marketing teams around the world will talk about how to prey on male vulnerability. It's so easy. Tell a man that he will seem stronger, or that women will like him more, or that he'll feel more at-ease, and he's much more likely to buy your product.

It's also easy to get men and boys to join a political movement if it takes away those complications and doubts. Charismatic figures that offer a way for men to feel good about themselves will always attract a following of vulnerable men and boys. We saw this with the Andrew Tate phenomenon - an objectively average man who, because he offered a simple rhetoric to men that promised money, power, sex and self-esteem, became famous. He only had to fall back into the language of undiluted patriarchy, and have the confidence to say things that most people find repulsive, and he was able to capture the imaginations of men around the world. I know several teachers who tell me that the boys in their class all know who Andrew Tate is, and they quote him, going as far as attacking their female teachers.

What many men are seeking, above all, is relief. They're looking for things that will take the uncertainty away, they're looking for simple answers that make them feel better about themselves, which promise a simple route to the things they yearn for. Emotional needs tend to play a much larger part in our decision making than we want to admit, and for men who haven't found their own belief structure, there is a constant emotional pressure to find reassuring answers to their problems.

MENTAL ILLNESS

We're at our best when the majority of our intrinsic needs are met, and we tend to become unwell if important needs go unsatisfied for a long time. This can show up as unhappiness, poor physical health, low self-esteem, addictive behaviour...or a hundred other things. One common side effect of long-term unmet needs is mental health issues.

We all need some simple things like meaningful connection with other people, a feeling of basic safety, a sense of purpose, the knowledge that we're contributing positively to the world, belonging within a community that feels good, and some acknowledgement and respect for the person we are and the things we do.

If a man feels like he's constantly failing, or he doesn't know how to earn respect and position, or his instincts and early-life programming are telling him to believe things, feel things and do things that consistently fail to bring him the results that he craves in life, or if he feels trapped between strong conflicting perspectives on masculinity, or any other daily personal hardship that comes from living in a patriarchal culture...he may well end up with mental health problems. Depression or anxiety are common in these situations, as are addiction and even fixating on the idea of suicide.

In these situations, it's really helpful for a man to consider how much of his psychological pain comes from his early life programming. Maybe it's not him at all, it's just stuff that he was taught when he was young, or stuff that he's picked up along the way. It's really normal for people to have beliefs that have no basis in reality, and which lead us to making really dumb or counter-productive choices all the time. Any man who has ongoing mental health challenges should consider this, and try to expose himself to feminist thought and, wherever possible, hire a good therapist to heal whatever's lurking under the surface and causing his struggles.

RESTRICTION OF CHOICE AND EXPRESSION IN MEN AND WOMEN

Patriarchal culture tells us all what we should be. Men should be this, women should be that, and we should all feel shame if we fall short of these standards.

Both men and women who have internalised patriarchal beliefs will have strong opinions about how men and women should behave, how they should look, what they should do with their time, what jobs they should have, and what role they should have in a relationship or a family. You know it's programming rather than a deeply considered opinion when your emotional response to someone breaking the rules is immediate and strong.

If you ever see somebody doing something and you immediately feel an overwhelming emotion like anger, rage, revulsion, disgust, contempt or loathing, then you're almost certainly being driven by a belief that was implanted in you as a child.

This shapes our thinking. We don't want to have those strong emotions, so we avoid thinking about some things, and we make assumptions about the world so that we don't have to deal with the emotional turbulence of confronting how the world really is. We will let ourselves believe things about what women and men should do, and we'll be careful not to think about it too deeply.

Nobody likes to think of themselves as programmed, or manipulated, or prejudiced, or bigoted. The most prejudiced people in the world will tell themselves that they're not. Many misogynists will say they are pro-women, they love women, they work really hard to support women. What they mean is, as long as women behave themselves and fit into narrow confines, I will love and support them. If they want to be anything other than what I expect, I will despise or attack them.

Victims or patriarchal programming are not ok with men being emotional, or men being expressive, or men pursuing creative careers or hobbies, or gay, bi or trans men, or men who choose to be a stay-at-home dad.

Equally, people with strong patriarchal programming will not be ok with vocal, powerful women, or women who work as engineers, mechanics, soldiers or other traditionally male jobs, or women who hold men to high standards, or lesbian, bi or trans women, or women who don't exhibit a caring, nurturing persona.

We tend not to notice how our beliefs and prejudices manipulate our freedom of choice, but these are some examples. Earlier I mentioned the idea of conscious living, and a key part of this is coming to terms with the web of beliefs that restricts your choices, and freeing yourself from them. Anyone who has strong feelings about what men and women *should* do, should consider how free they are.

PERFORMATIVE AESTHETICS

I enjoy a lot of fitness training, and I lift weights. It has loads of health benefits and I like to feel good about how I look. However, if you're living an unconscious life where you're motivated by a lot of unconscious beliefs, it's easy to lose your way with your appearance.

So many men today are obsessed with their appearance. Many men train obsessively at the gym, and diet heavily, and chase the Hollywood action hero body. They often spend a lot of money on skin products and training supplements.

What's going on here is that these guys are chasing the satisfaction of the needs for connection, belonging, respect and acknowledgement, and they've been taught, at some point in their lives, that they need to be 'manly' to achieve these things. Somewhere along the way they've mixed up potency and personal power with the idea of looking like an action hero. They believe they should look like the guys on TV and they believe that doors will open for them if they do (for example, women will want to sleep with them). Therefore they feel a huge pressure to starve themselves, use lots of products, and train obsessively.

I don't want to knock professional athletes here, I'm specifically talking about men who have a burning need to look a very certain way, and until they do they feel ashamed and it really impacts their self-esteem. Equally, when they hit that dream percentage of body fat, or when they flex and see rippling muscles, they can get a big hit of satisfaction. They've made it! They can finally feel proud of themselves. Other men develop body dysmorphia and no matter how far their six-pack stands out, what they see in the mirror is a fat ugly failure.

Both women and men can fall victim to this, of course. Women have always starved themselves, gone through painful procedures or hated themselves for not looking pretty enough. That's patriarchy telling a woman that her value as a human being is her attractiveness to men. Men have now joined in, and over the last few decades we've seen an explosion of men chasing a certain appearance in order to feel good about themselves.

VENERATION OF VIOLENCE

Patriarchy tells men that they should be dominant, powerful, virile and in-control, and it has no moral qualms about men using violence to achieve this. 19th Century historians invented this idea of brutal cave men who ruled through violence, where only the strongest men got to mate with the women. It's pure fabrication (there was a huge variety of pre-modern cultures around the world, many of which were matriarchal or pacifist), but it lingers on in our collective imagination, and it seems to give legitimacy to the idea of brutal men who take what they want. At the time of writing this, Andrew Tate is having an enormous influence on teenage boys around the world. A lot of school teachers are hearing boys using Tate-like language, and being dismissive or abusive towards female teachers.

Fewer men today would openly talk about using violence to get what they want, but domestic violence is still common, a leading cause of death amongst women is still their male partners, and vulnerable young men can still venerate murderers and psychopaths.

EXPECTATION, PRIVILEGE AND LEARNED HELPLESSNESS

Patriarchy teaches men that they are superior to women, that they should have the power and dominance, and that women are 'other' and not entirely human. This has some strange knock-on effect in men's thinking, if they're not careful and if they're not self aware.

Many can believe, unconsciously, that they deserve to receive things in life, like power, status, respect, success and money. They can feel something is wrong with the world if they don't have these things, they might make choices based on the expectation that they'll receive these things, and they can get very frustrated and angry if they don't receive them. They might also look at women receiving these things and feel like something is wrong with that.

Parents who raise their kids under patriarchal beliefs might also pass on some expectations that are easy to miss. Most women I have known will clean their homes regularly, even if they're exhausted, and especially if guests are coming to visit. Many men I've known never think about this, and let dishes pile up, let kitchen surfaces get dirty, especially if they're very tired from a long day. If you ignore patriarchy, you might conclude that women are just naturally more fastidious than men. A lot of people think this. Women are obsessed with keeping things clean and women will push themselves to clear or provide for their kids where a man will just flop on the couch. This also extends (I believe) to this idea that women can multitask better than men. Again, this is easy to explain by saying that women's brains are just better at that. As far as I know, there's no evidence to support this idea.

Rather, girls are just expected to do all this. In many homes, girls are expected to clean the home, no matter how tired they are. Girls are expected to be able to remember and process many things at once, where boys are let off from needing to do this. I'm not saying that girls have a harder childhood than boys (that will depend on the household), but in the same way that boys aren't taught about emotions, they aren't held to high standards in things like cleaning, caring, cooking or things related to maintaining the home. I don't believe that women are better at multitasking, I simply believe that girls are expected to remember more things at once, so they learn to do it. I don't believe that women care more about having clean homes simply because they're women, I believe that patriarchy tells women that their self-worth is linked to a clean home, so no matter how tired they are, they must clean.

Bad solutions

So many men in our society have inherited toxic programming and bad lessons, and most of these men have no idea that their true, authentic selves are being warped and poisoned by this programming. However, underneath it all is a healthy human being who wants to form connections, find purpose and belonging, and share himself with the world.

Men who are still dominated by patriarchal conditioning will feel that something is wrong. Life doesn't feel right. However, instead of looking inwards and questioning the things they've been taught, they will often blame other people or the world in general. This makes sense. Patriarchy is designed for a world where men have all the power, where women only exist as accessories to men's pleasure and success, where men smother and crush their own emotional needs and where a man knowns clearly whether he's succeeding or failing (and his success is the measure of his worth as a human being). This world has been progressively dismantled over the past century and now the beliefs that still exist within many men no longer make sense in the real world.

This disconnect between a man's expectation and the world he actually finds will cause him frustration, distress and emotional pain. In the next section of the book, I'll explain how men can escape this programming and heal their wounds, which makes all the pain go away and escapes all the effects that we've looked at already.

However, millions of men are experiencing this, and that creates opportunities for bad actors. Alongside the things that genuinely help (listed in the next section), there are things that claim to be solutions, but which actually make the problem worse. Some of these are:

PROUD MISOGYNISTS

If your beliefs about how the world *should be* don't fit with how the world actually is, it'll always be easy for people to convince you that you're right and the world is wrong. Men with patriarchal conditioning need to heal things within themselves (that's always true), but this is a difficult, emotionally challenging thing to do, and patriarchy doesn't want them to do it.

So, a lot of men won't make this choice. The main reasons why are:

- They're enjoying the privilege they're receiving
- They're too wounded to be able to see the extent of their wounding
- A lack of influences and role models that might inspire them to liberate themselves
- They're too afraid of what might happen if they lift the lid on their emotions and do the work to understand themselves

This means that we all know proud misogynists: men who revel in how obnoxious they are, and who have constructed an elaborate belief system that lets them keep being proudly and blatantly toxic.

These men can have a ripple effect on men around them, giving permission to stay toxic and hostile to women. It can feel like relief from the inner torment of being trapped between conflicting world-views, and so many men find these misogynists funny and endearing.

What they deserve, of course, is pity, scepticism and education. They're unable to free themselves from a belief structure that's way out-of-date, which harms themselves and every woman they meet, and which keeps them from becoming an authentic, balanced human being.

EXPLOITATIVE LEADERS

It's so easy to get elected if you tap into populist and patriarchal language. From the union at work to the highest office in the land, if you can speak directly to people's pain they will believe anything and hand you power. Unscrupulous men have always known this, and they use it to their advantage. There will always be people who want simple answers that might cause harm to people, rather than complex answers that demand some introspection, and these people will vote for exploitative leaders.

No matter how emotionally connected you feel with a leader, make sure you interrogate their beliefs carefully. As we've seen, many men think of themselves as feminists or at least as supporters of women, and yet they'll reject women's humanity and their freedom to choose their own path. Always ask: do the leaders that you support truly want balance between genders, and do they act like they believe women are real people, or are women just accessories to them?

PRODUCT MARKETING

It's so easy to sell things to people who are suffering, if you sell them the possibility of relief. Men who are clinging to patriarchal beliefs, who feel this sense of *wrongness* in the world, will carry an unconscious discomfort through their day, and marketers know this. They design products that will speak to a man's frustration, confusion or insecurity.

Any product that's designed to make a man feel more 'manly' would fall into this category. This could really be anything, from a car to a pair of jeans, to cologne to cosmetic surgery. These products will try to use language, colours or imagery that evoke the idea of masculinity.

Sometimes this can be harmless in the world, but falling for this trap will always be a step in the wrong direction. Men need to do the work, come home to their authenticity and liberate themselves from their programming. Each time you spend money on something to reinforce your masculinity, you're telling yourself that it isn't secure.

PATRIARCHAL RELIGIONS

Religion and spiritual life can play a massive part in people's healing and growth, but like everywhere else, there will be bad actors who are either trapped in patriarchal programming themselves, or who are using the distress of men to exploit them.

Christianity and other Abrahamic faiths emerged out of cultures that are very different to ours, and we'd reject many things that they say. During my time studying theology, I learned that we have only the vaguest idea of what the bible actually says, given the mistakes, misunderstandings and prejudices that crept into translation between Hebrew, Greek and English, and because of how much politics was involved in some of the big edits. There's also a wide variety of approaches to interpreting what a religion tells us, but almost everyone agreed that you need to compromise. We don't tend to think that people wearing clothes made of different fibres are sinful and immoral, even though this is written in the bible. We've moved beyond the idea that slavery is acceptable, but the ancient writings of many religions make reference to slavery and seem to have no problem with it. All religions pick and choose which things they hold sacrosanct and which things they re-interpret.

This should make us really sceptical of religious leaders and groups who choose to keep any patriarchal views. Why would you do that? Why give men primacy, or deny the personhood and freedom of women, or create different standards of behaviour for men and women? We should all focus on the real motivations of anyone who chooses to do this, because they're probably not healthy and they're probably not interested in the truth.

How all this shows up in men

I want to take a moment to say that I'm being really simplistic here. I'm reducing millions of men to simple chunks of theory. I'm doing that because it's helpful when we're trying to understand why men do hurtful things to themselves and others, and why there seem to be these consistent patterns in men's words and actions.

Men, of course, are just people. At any one time, about half of my coaching clients are men and the reason my job is so exciting and so fascinating is that everyone I meet is a bottomless, mysterious world of experiences and beliefs and emotions and ideas and I feel so hugely privileged to get access to it all. My male clients are just as fascinating as my female clients, with exactly the same level of complexity and depth.

However, we've all known plenty of men who have been reduced to just a stereotype by the conditioning of their early lives. It's tragic. I see them unable to share their inner worlds with anyone, I see the loneliness this has baked into their lives, I see the impossible standards they're trying to live up to, I see the counter-productive strategies they develop, and I see the resentment, hostility and vulnerability that's lurking behind their tough exterior.

So, sadly, a lot of men do fall into predictable types, at least in the way they go about dating, or relating to women, or having sex. Behind every Misogynist, every User, every Timebomb, is a rich and intriguing person with complex feelings and depth, but the women these men date won't often get to see it.

You'll find my list of 10 types of toxic men in part three of this book. Within each type, I've tried to describe them accurately, to unpack how their psychology leads to their weird or hurtful behaviour, what each type needs to do in order to heal, and then a section about why women are attracted to these types of men and what *they* need to do to heal.

It's not women's job to rescue wounded men

It's really easy for women to take on the role of a rescuer in a relationship. Perhaps she sees her partner struggling, deeply unhappy, stuck in repeating cycles or unable to communicate his thoughts and feelings.

Women who have done some personal development work, or who have a clearer insight into psychology than the men she knows, will often slip into the trap of rescuing men. Especially partners. There aren't many other options, when you realise that your partner is in psychological pain and unable to free themselves from their programming. You can put up with their behaviour, even if it hurts you or degrades the quality of your life. You can leave and try to find someone who isn't a victim to such programming. Or you can try to fix him, and many women feel a lot of pressure to fix him.

This might look like:

- Dreaming about how good it could be, and thinking a lot about how close things are to being better. If only he was able to see the things I can see! It would make the relationship easier, happier, more fulfilling for both of us.

- A feeling of obligation. If I'm committed to this relationship then I should help him to get through things. It's my duty to support him.

- Deciding that there's nothing better out there, that all men are like this.

- Buying him lots of books or trying to get him to watch TED talks or listen to podcasts.

- Making excuses to other people for his behaviour.

If you're committed to a relationship then it's wonderful to support your partner, and we all need a little support sometimes. The risk here is that a combination of internalised patriarchy (women's duty to be carers and mothers) with any personal issues around needing to rescue other people can keep women trapped in relationships they don't want. If you ever lose your freedom to choose because you're being driven by an unconscious need to rescue your partner from their own demons, then something has gone wrong. You can end up validating and encouraging his dependency on you, and you can tolerate things from him that you know you shouldn't.

It's tricky to find the line when being supportive trips over into rescuing behaviour. If you ever think you might have crossed this line, here's some advice to get clarity around your motivations:

- Ask yourself: do I feel an obligation to save, fix or change him?

- If yes, where does that feeling of obligation come from?

- If you feel like it's worth 'sticking it out' until things get better, create a clear picture in your mind of what 'better' looks like. Write it down and regularly check that things are getting closer to that 'better' world. Where strong emotions are involved, we can easily keep moving the goalposts to give ourselves more time or tolerate a lack of progress.

- Are there things that you feel you aren't allowed to say to your partner? If yes, where do these fears come from?

PART TWO: HOPE AND HEALING

Healing in men

So many women in my life have talked to me about horrible men they've known, from neglectful men, or distant men who just didn't know how to communicate, to men who treated them like toys to be played with, to men who were actively abusive or violent. The stories are consistent: women report the same things over and over. We also have the core theory, which I've been exploring in the last part of this book, around developmental psychology and the nature of patriarchy. I've not invented anything new in this book, this is stuff you would learn in any good psychology degree.

The theory and evidence line up really neatly. To me the conclusion is obvious: so many men have their emotions and thoughts warped by their early-life indoctrination, and this leads to all the strange behaviour and unhappiness we see in men. The world is also structured to keep men trapped/protected in this indoctrination. There is enough privilege left, and there are enough stereotypes remaining, that men can still lose themselves in the rewarding side of patriarchy while ignoring the poisonous effects it's having on them, on the men around them, and on the women they meet.

In this chapter, I'm going to talk about the healing process, because this is not a hopeless situation. As I've said already, and as I'll continue to say, there's nothing inherently wrong with men. Men are just people; they're complex, interesting, they can be wonderful partners, parents, friends and leaders. Some men have grown up with some beliefs that limit their freedom, which cause them harm, and which encourage them to cause harm to others…but so have most women. We all grow up with problematic things lurking at the back of our minds, picked up from one source or another.

If you're a man who wants to heal what was done to him, or if you know a man who needs healing, here is some guidance…

Finding you own reason to begin

Everyone needs their own reason to begin working on personal development and growth. If your reason resonates with you emotionally, you'll be willing to notice, confront and overcome things within yourself. Many people get into self-help because of vague curiosity: a friend recommends a book that changed their life, or work puts you on through a workshop or exercise which teaches you things about yourself and it leaves you curious to know more.

Many people, however, need a push. Most people's reason to begin personal work is obvious, compelling and clear.

Personal development means facing things you usually avoid. It means recognising and understanding difficult things within yourself. It means learning all sorts of things about the way human beings work. It's not quick, it's often emotionally challenging, it's a world full of grifters and bad actors, and a lot of people are deeply sceptical about it. Those are just some of the reasons people avoid doing the work.

And yet, there are so many important things that we're not taught about how to live happy lives, and in the absence of some kind of wise elder caste, all we have to fall back on is self-help, philosophy, spiritual traditions, therapists and life coaches.

In this book we've looked at the ways that Patriarchy stops men from asking for help, for fear of being mocked or feeling like a failure as a man. So men tend to need a really strong motivation to take their first steps into self exploration. If a man doesn't find a compelling reason to begin, he'll quickly quit, or won't get very far.

So my first piece of advice is for a man to find his own strong motivation to begin personal development work.

Here are some things that often motivate men to begin:

- I want to stop repeating patterns in relationships which always seem to end the same way and I don't know why.

- I want to be much happier than I've ever been. I think I'm held back by things inside me, or I'm being made unhappy by things in my head or in my heart. I want to understand and fix those things.

- I want to understand myself very deeply so I know I'm being the best possible partner to the woman I love.

- I want to be a good father, which might mean…

  ◦ I want to shield my children from the stuff I inherited from my own father

  ◦ I want to be emotionally present and expressive with my children so they grow up to be balanced people

  ◦ I want to ensure my son grows up to be a good man who understands himself and who is a good influence in the world.

  ◦ I want to be able to connect with my daughter and understand what she's facing as she goes through school and enters the world as a young woman.

- I sometimes do things that aren't good, that I'm not proud of, and I can't seem to stop myself and I hate it. (this might be things like addiction, saying things you don't mean, people pleasing, being abusive or falling into a depression and withdrawing from all your friends)

- I want to be sure I'm reaching my potential, and not being held back by mental or emotional problems I've developed somewhere in my life.

- I've been told I'm not good at expressing my feelings or being empathetic, and I want to develop those skills.

Therapy

There are a lot of forms of psychotherapy and coaching these days, and there's a reason that talking therapies have become a multi-billion dollar industry. While there's still a lot of stigma and suspicion around therapy, many people have now found that investing in a good therapist is a hugely positive, life-changing experience. We all have baggage, we all have psychological wounds that we need to explore and resolve. That's a universal thing shared by all people - the world that we all grew up in bruises us all in different ways, and resolving those bruises leaves us with more positive feelings, more energy and clearer thinking.

Talking to friends and family is great, but it's not the same. We all, at some point in our lives, need a well-trained professional in a dedicated space, to go through a healing process. It's exactly like speaking to a doctor to heal a physical problem.

Therapy is simply the most efficient and effective way to explore and understand yourself. You're hiring someone whose job is to help you, and you're making a personal commitment by spending the money. That means everyone involved has a vested interest in making progress. Loads of other things in life will help you grow and develop (running a business, running a marathon, climbing a mountain, travelling to other cultures, having a child) but those are all chaotic: they may or may not give you insights and breakthroughs. You might find the information you need, you might have a conversation that helps you understand things in a new way, or you might not. Therapy is more effective because it's tailored to one purpose: your understanding, your psychological healing and your growth as a person.

What do you get out of therapy, exactly? Well, that varies from person to person, but common things are:

- A deeper understanding of why you feel the way you feel
- Improved skills in emotional communication and empathy, which lead to improvements in relationships, in parenting, in friendships, at work...
- Better at resolving conflicts
- New and better strategies to handle challenges in your life
- More certainty about who you are and what you want
- More of a sense of being in control
- Deeper fulfilment and more appreciation of the things in your life
- Resolving mental health challenges
- A deeper and more passionate experience of love and sex

In my experience, men tend to tell themselves stories about why they shouldn't engage in therapy. I've certainly told myself a lot of these, at times in my life where I've fought against the therapy

I needed. Here are some of the most common excuses men given themselves, along with my answers to each:

EXCUSES	
"Therapy is for crazy people, or people in much worse situations than me. I'm not suicidal, I'm not hearing voices, I don't need a therapist."	That's an old-fashioned view of therapy, and it's more about psychiatry than psychotherapy. You don't need to be in crisis to speak to a therapist, you just need a personal issue that you want to explore in a safe, structured, professional environment. Try reading or watching things about modern therapy and notice how it's not really about crazy people, it's just people who want to better themselves.
"Sure, maybe therapy works for other people but it wouldn't work for me." *or* "I don't need to try it, I know it's not for me." *or* "A therapist could never understand me."	These are the kind of vague things people tell themselves to avoid the feelings that are really stopping them from engaging in therapy. Normally this is a strong fear of something. If you decide not to engage in therapy because you're afraid, that's fine. But don't tell yourself stories just to avoid acknowledging your fear.

(continued on next page)

"If I lift the lid on my problems, they might spin out of control and I'll never be able to function again."	Yes, that's theoretically possible. If you are carefully managing your thoughts and feelings and you know that you'll lose control if you stop managing them in exactly this way, that's an important thing to know before you begin therapy. The answer is to begin gently. Begin by speaking to several therapists until you get a good feeling about someone who might be able to help you, and be sure to tell them about this fear you have so they can make the process gradual and safe for you. You always remain in control of the therapeutic process, so if things ever feel shaky or unsafe for you, tell your therapist and ask to proceed more gently.
"If my friends or family ever found out I was in therapy, I'd never live it down. I couldn't cope with their jokes, their judgement or their rejection."	I'm sorry your friendships are so conditional, and I'm sorry that you fear rejection by the people you love. Is it really true? Could you try speaking more frankly to them and see if they really reject you? And if they definitely would, just don't tell them. Plenty of people have therapy in secret.
"I'd feel like less of a man if I went to therapy"	This is a chicken and an egg situation. You believe that your manhood is dependent on going it alone, being completely independent, never asking for help. That's conditioning and wounding from your childhood that you could resolve through therapy. You're going to interrupt these beliefs so you can resolve the problems that are holding you back. It's your choice you have to make: you have the power to take control of your inner world.

If you search for therapists in your local area, you may be overwhelmed by the results. Often there are dozens and it can be difficult to choose. My main advice is: check their qualifications and experience, read their material thoroughly and ultimately, trust your gut. Speak to several people before you commit to someone. Go with someone who seems nice, who seems competent, and make sure you speak to them on the phone before your first session. If it just feels like a sales pitch, back off. You should feel good about someone before you try opening your mind and your heart to them.

After that, don't just go for one session. You can't know from one session whether someone is right for you. Try at least 2 or 3 sessions, then make your decision about sticking with them or trying someone else.

Chase authenticity

We are not talking here about making you into something you're not, we're talking about making you *more you*.

A man who decides to step away from patriarchal conditioning and become free will face a lot of obstacles, both around him and within him. People might judge you, if you decide to do this, and you will almost certainly find limiting beliefs within yourself. You might imagine that you're going to lose your strength, or you'll become like some people you don't like. Some men even fear that they will 'turn gay' or become effeminate and ineffective.

None of this needs to be true. What we're talking about here is the path of liberation. You are not the person you have been conditioned to be. Men who aren't able to access their feelings, or men who lose control of themselves in certain situations, or men who act abusively towards the women they love, or men who can be manipulated by people into giving up hobbies they love, or shamed into not speaking things that they know to be true… this is not freedom. This is a man in a trap. This is a man who is preventing themselves from discovering who they can truly be.

So I encourage men to hold onto this word: authenticity. As you learn about your early life programming and your cultural programming, try to move steadily further towards your true self. Ask yourself, each time you find yourself at a decision point: which road will take me further towards my most authentic self?

Exposure to other points of view

One of the great limiters on our ability to fully embrace our lives is all the things we don't know that we don't know. We grow up in a place, in a family, and we go through a certain education. We get told some things, but when we enter adulthood we probably only have a tiny fraction of the knowledge that we could have.

It's easy to live a small life, unaware of all the things we don't know, often missing ideas or answers that could change everything for us. We tell ourselves that this is what life is. We believe that people think the way we think, feel the way we feel and believe the things we believe. Increasingly, we've been encouraged to see people who are different to us as the enemy, as idiots and sometimes, as less than human.

So it's never been more important to intentionally seek out fresh perspectives on things. Men should research what it feels like to be a woman at this time, or to be a minority group. Try to read things from their point of view. Men should travel, with the intention of learning things from new cultures. Try to escape tired ideas of cultural superiority - people in other cultures have things to teach you.

Essentially: go looking for fresh ways to see everything. Intentionally take yourself out of your comfort zone and see what's out there. Go with humility and a willingness to learn, to be wrong, to discover things you didn't know that you didn't know.

Good role models

The world is full of wonderful role models for men who are trying to liberate themselves from their conditioning. These might be wholesome men who have already walked the path and freed themselves, or it can be powerful women who will challenge your assumptions and compel you to level-up.

If you are a man on this journey, go looking for role models who:

- You can respect
- Speak with respect about everyone
- Form healthy relationships, and speak openly about them
- Regularly challenge your assumptions and forces you to think again
- Bring fresh learning and information into your life
- Embody the kind of person you'd love to be

Active Listening skills

One of the things that patriarchal indoctrination teaches men is that it's their role to solve problems. In the right setting, this is fine. We all need to be strong, independent people who carry a solution-oriented mindset. We all need to be good at identifying and solving problems. Those skills are an asset.

The problem is that men will tend to see every conversation about problems as a conversation about solutions, and that's not always true. There are conversations about problems that require solutions and there are conversations about problems which are just about sharing our challenges and getting some relief because we know we've been heard. Often, when people are talking about struggles and problems, what they're really looking for is listening and recognition, not solutions. If you offer solutions in these conversations, it feels crap for the speaker. They didn't get what they needed from the conversation.

This is part of a broader problem. Men can find emotional conversations scary or exhausting, because they weren't taught how to deal with these kinds of situations as a kid. They didn't develop instincts to deal with emotional conversations, so it requires their conscious mind to really focus and respond effectively. Without realising it, many men tend to just want any deep conversation to be over, so they offer practical advice to make the conversation go away, or they zone out, or they intentionally say the wrong thing so their partner gives up trying to communicate with them.

Some intrinsic needs are belonging, and recognition, and feeling heard and respected in relationships. We all need these things, to some degree. If someone isn't getting those needs satisfied when they speak to you, they will feel like you don't care or that you can't connect with them. It will make a relationship unsatisfying, stale and difficult.

Men can develop listening skills. There's nothing about men that makes them bad listeners, it's just a lack of practice. So men: treat listening like going to the gym. You need to strengthen this muscle by putting in the work. Research the techniques of *active listening*, online and in books. When someone is talking to you, bring your full focus to bear and don't let yourself take an easy way out. Listen, try to empathise with what's being said, and respond from your heart. It may be that none of those skills were taught in your childhood, so you're starting from scratch here. But put the work in, get strong in this area. Your partner will love it.

Emotional skills

Emotions get a bad rap in Western culture. They're easily dismissed as useless, erratic, childish or dangerous. Sure, they can be those things but your emotions are a massive part of your life. Everything you appreciate most in life is emotional.

Emotions will be with you, for every moment of every day, whether you notice them or not. At the very least, you need to manage and express them in ways that give you great results. At best, skillful emotional management and empathy skills will transform your relationships, your sex life, your friendships, your work, your parenting, and how much you enjoy each moment of your life.

The expert I respect most in this field is Karla McLaren. Her core book, The Language of Emotions, is big and I've never known a man to find it an easy read.

McLaren doesn't see emotions are mad or unpredictable, she sees them as essential messengers from a deep and wise part of us. Often our emotions tell us things that our conscious mind hasn't figured out yet. It turns out that each emotion has a specific purpose, and once we understand that purpose, and how to harness it, each emotion becomes a superpower that we've got access to.

When I coach men who are still hostile towards the very idea of emotions, I see somebody who's willfully making their life worse. It's like going through life with one eye closed. Everyone around you has two eyes, so you're immediately at a disadvantage, and they generally won't understand why you've done this to yourself. A lot of these men go through life feeling like they're better than other people because they don't get involved with their feelings, when really they are hamstrung, disadvantaged, limited and held back by their lack of skill.

This is almost a universal problem. The patriarchal stigma against understanding and expressing your emotions affects almost all men, to some degree. So all men could do with an education in developing emotional skills. Research it, find teachers or experts who speak your language and see it as a learning opportunity rather than something that will undermine your masculinity. A man who understands his feelings, a man with skills in emotional communication and empathy, doesn't become weak. Ditch those stereotypes. Emotional men are stronger than unemotional men.

Healthy brotherhood

If you're a man interested in healing and becoming wiser and stronger, you might initially feel very alone. You may know a lot of men who are still trapped by their patriarchal programming. The feeling of being alone, or rejected, or abandoned, is one of the main things that stops men from exploring the fullness of their humanity.

I'd encourage all men to seek our brothers in this work. This might be mentors who can guide you, it might be friends who are also curious about breaking free, or it might be a group of men who are doing this together. Increasingly, there are men's circles in most major towns and cities. Make sure this feels like a safe and wholesome space, because there are also plenty of men's groups which are designed to double-down on patriarchy, men who actively poison one another into being even more hostile towards women. But there are also men who are growing their emotional skills, men who want to be real and authentic with one another. If you can't find brothers locally, perhaps look online for a place you can speak with other men doing this work.

If at all possible, don't walk this path alone.

Healthy habits

There will be big decisions and moments for any man who walks this journey, but the things that really add up are the little things you do every day, or every week. Changes in feeling or belief are great, but until they show up in changes of behaviour you're not really making lasting changes.

Good habits for anyone who is engaged in personal development include:

- Some form of meditation, to train your brain
- Regular journaling of your thoughts and feelings
- Reading interesting books that broaden your horizons and challenge your assumptions
- Limit your phone use, and put your phone out of sight during conversations, meals and social time
- Walks in nature with no distractions or purpose
- Setting and completing meaningful challenges: run that marathon, jump out that plane, learn that language
- Practise conscious gratitude (regularly take time to list things in your mind that you feel genuinely grateful for)

A couple of good books in this area are Atomic Habits by James Clear and The Power of Habit by Charles Duhigg.

Healing in women

Here, I just want to remind any women reading this book that you may have your own healing to do. One of my closest friends is a formidable feminist and activist, but for years in our conversation she would, without noticing what she was doing, talk about physically beautiful women being better than less attractive women. It showed up during our conversations, without her realising it, and I'd sometimes point it out (yes, I'm pretty annoying as a friend sometimes). Now, she's labelled that part of herself as her own internalised patriarchy and she's working to flush it out and stop listening to it. Patriarchy, of course, teaches us all that women's greatest value is their usefulness and attractiveness to men, and so many women carry fragments of internalised patriarchy in the unconscious belief that their worth is tied to their attractiveness. Women's self-esteem can be badly damaged by unrecognised beliefs like this.

The other main reason to continue 'doing the work' would be the kind of men you're attracted to.

It's so common for women to date the same kind of toxic men over and over, and eventually come to the conclusion that all men must be toxic. If you find yourself meeting the same behaviour in the men you date, I'd encourage you to be curious about what in you is seeking out the traits that these men offer. Their toxicity is not your fault, and I'm not suggesting that you're to blame, but if certain toxic traits excite you then that might be something to investigate in therapy. Many women are attracted to men who are arrogant, or insulting, or sexually aggressive, or emotionally distant, or even violent. It's good to understand why these things are attractive or exciting for you, and if you find that it's the result of early-life conditioning, or if a part of your is trying to recreate a relationship that felt loving and safe in your past (but was in fact, quite toxic or problematic) then that's a thing to try to resolve through personal development work.

So, many women have work to do. A wonderful recent book in this field is Fix the System, Not the Women by Laura Bates. Books like this, and so many other feminist books, can help keep you motivated and give you ideas and direction for your own healing.

Attachment styles

Attachment Theory is a well-researched and developed area of psychology, and it's something I'd encourage everyone to learn about. A good book about this is Attachment Theory by Thais Gibson.

The theory is that our early life relationships, usually with our parents, teach us things that we take into our adult romantic relationships. There are only a few 'attachment styles' and when you know yours, it gives you a huge amount of information about why you do certain things in relationships, and also it helps you recognise your partner's habits and needs.

Whoever you are, please ensure you know your attachment style, and if you're in a relationship make sure you know your partner's attachment style too.

Green Flags: What does healthy even look like?

With all this talk of patriarchy, programming, toxic behaviour and psychological wounding, it's easy to lose sight of all the amazing men in the world and their traits. As I keep saying, there's nothing inherently wrong with men. The problem is patriarchy.

Healthy men, and men who are in the process of healing, are everywhere. Few men have entirely freed themselves from early-life programming and patriarchal culture, but many men are on that journey. These men tend to be freer, safer, more reliable, more interesting and better at connecting than unconscious men.

So here are some green flags to look out for if you want a man who's going to make a great partner:

HE ADMITS WHEN HE'S WRONG, HE'S ABLE TO SAY SORRY, HE SAYS "I DON'T KNOW" WHEN HE DOESN'T KNOW

While men with a strong sense of identity and purpose will often have interesting opinions on things, it's a good sign if he occasionally says he doesn't know the answer to something. It shows he's being open and honest. Equally, he sometimes needs to demonstrate an ability to admit when he's in the wrong about something, because that shows a strong character that isn't destabilised by being proven wrong.

HE SEEMS AT EASE IN HIMSELF, PHYSICALLY RELAXED

This is a sign of psychological health in a man. He's fine with himself, he's pretty at ease going about his day, the life that he's built will feel good to him, and this comfort will show up in his body and posture. He'll seem relaxed and comfortable in his own skin.

HE ASKS YOUR OPINION ABOUT THINGS

Even men who have done a lot of work on themselves fall into this trap. They'll believe they're kind and decent, but they'll never ask women their opinions about things, or ask them for advice. They're still unconsciously biassed towards believing men know better. It's a great sign when a man shows a genuine and consistent interest in your opinions, without needing to remind himself that he should. He's telling you things about what he believes.

HE'S CONSISTENT

This is a real mark of maturity and stability in a man. He'll seem emotionally consistent, he'll be consistent in the things he says, he'll feel like the same person no matter who's around. Men who still have plenty of work to do on themselves will struggle with this. They might be emotionally erratic, or change their stories or views on things, or change their identity to fit in with people and situations.

HE HAS A GOOD HISTORY OF RELATIONSHIPS, FRIENDSHIPS AND TEAMWORK

Does he have a healthy past or is there a history of conflict, dysfunction or confusion? Does he speak well of his exes, or does he complain about them? Does he seem to understand the idea that a relationship is a team, and can you see that he's demonstrated teamwork in the past?

HE'S HONEST, OPEN, AND ABLE TO BE VULNERABLE

He doesn't need to tell you everything about everything, we're all allowed our privacy and we're all allowed to protect the privacy of others, but a healthy man will be fine being open and honest about most topics. He speaks the truth and doesn't lie. When he's uncomfortable, challenged, upset or otherwise emotionally triggered, he can be vulnerable and express himself, rather than simply use a coping mechanism that keeps him emotionally walled-off.

HE HAS A SENSE OF DIRECTION (THE RELATIONSHIP IS NOT HIS TOP PRIORITY)

As strange as it may seem, relationships are at their best when they aren't a man's top priority. He'll have his own goals, or passions, or dreams. The relationship makes his life better, makes him better, lends his life more depth and joy, but without it he would still have direction and purpose. This is a sign of a man with strength of character, of a man who has reflected deeply, committed to things, and built up resilience to the challenges and pitfalls of pursuing a purpose in life. All great things to look for in a partner.

HE'S ENGAGED IN SOME KIND OF ONGOING PERSONAL WORK

Most of us need to work on ourselves in some way, and this entire book is about how men usually have very specific beliefs and challenges that they need to overcome. So it's a great sign when a man is engaged in therapy, or coaching, or reading personal development books.

HE IS KIND, ESPECIALLY WHERE HE HAS NOTHING TO GAIN

It's easy to be kind to people when you're going to get something back (looking like a great guy, or being owed a favour, or tax breaks from charitable contributions). When a man is kind to someone with no chance of reward, he's demonstrating maturity and character. For him, being kind is just something you do, not something performative or a transaction. Kindness is a core character trait in a great partner.

There is always hope

One of the core beliefs in personal development, and one belief that all good therapists and coaches have in common, is that underneath our issues and confusion, we all have a healthy, whole, authentic self that we can return to. Most of us have lost our way to some degree, either through painful or unhelpful things in our childhoods, or traumas or bad experiences since, or through the way that life and our choices have shaped us. Ultimately we're all just trying to satisfy that inescapable list of mental and emotional needs in the best way we know how, but everyone picks up bad lessons, or fears of things, or counterproductive strategies along the way. It's up to each of us to look within ourselves for these limiting factors and work to resolve them.

Decades of therapeutic research and experience have shown that behind everyone's complexities, eccentricities and wounded behaviour, there is a happy and healthy person waiting to be reclaimed. We can all heal, we can all learn, we can all grow into someone stronger, smarter and wiser. Increasingly, people in senior positions around the world have learned that reaching their full potential means engaging in personal growth, therapy and enriching habits.

We've explored the epidemic of patriarchal conditioning that leads so many men to live small and stunted lives, and which can lead them towards toxic behaviour in relationships. All men can heal this stuff, and all women can shake off their own internalised patriarchy so they stop contributing to the problem.

I have written a series of books, called the Arete Trilogy, for anyone interested in understanding themselves deeply and engaging in lifelong growth. I've poured decades of learning and experience into it, from my time in training and academia, to meetings and board rooms and gyms, to my many years of clinical practice as a coach. If you're interested in a full understanding about who you are and what you need to do to thrive in every area of your life, I recommend you check out this series of books.

In the next section I'll unpack the 10 types of toxic men in relationships, and we'll take all this theory about patriarchy and healing into individual case studies and see the ways it shapes specific men into toxic parodies of their full, authentic selves.

PART THREE: 10 TYPES OF TOXIC MEN

How the 10 types work

Next, we're going to explore the most common ways that toxic beliefs and behaviour show up in men in our culture. I've talked a lot about how men are not inherently toxic, men are just people. However, as I've said, the programming that men receive in our culture limits them and stops them expressing themselves freely. This means that men who haven't 'done the work' to free themselves will fall into predictable types and patterns, which means that creating 10 common 'types' of toxic men is pretty easy.

The goal of this book is personal healing and freedom from limiting beliefs, with the hope that we can all find better, happier relationships. Even men who fit perfectly into one or more of these types can notice what's been done to them, and learn to come home to their authentic selves.

At the same time, we shouldn't pity these men - no matter what mental or emotional programming anyone is carrying, we all remain responsible for our words, choices and actions. So while there is always the possibility of healing and a change of behaviour, it must be a conscious choice. A man cannot be healed by others, and he can't be 'saved' or 'rescued' by other

Men can fall into several types at once. A man can be a Misogynist (Type 1), a User (Type 2) and a Lost Boy (Type 8) at the same time.

Also, the intensity of toxic behaviour in men will vary. Some Misogynists are obvious, loud and horrible to women wherever they find them, while others just mutter under their breath about stupid women all the time.

For each type, you'll read:

- A description of this type of man
- The red flags to watch out for
- The reason these men are dangerous to women
- A summary of the psychology that drives these men
- An explanation of the healing these men need
- Some words about why women would be attracted to men like this

As you read:

- Think about men you've known like this
- See if you can find a new way of seeing them
- For women: if you notice that, yes, you've dated or married this type of man, or if you've found them attractive in the past, be open to learning why this behaviour would attract you and think about what growth or healing you might need to do

- For men: if you feel some of these types describe some of your worst traits, just take that as a reminder that you still have work to do

THE 10 TYPES

Type 1: Misogynists

There are a lot of Misogynists in the world. You will find them in every profession and in many homes. The thing that makes them unique is their hostility towards women. A Misogynist will attack, insult, mock, humiliate and abuse women and see nothing wrong with doing so. He sees a woman's value purely in her usefulness to him: if they're attractive to him then they have some value, or if they make his life easier in some way. Otherwise, women are just the targets of his disdain.

The same psychology that makes him hostile towards women also leads him to be competitive with other men, so you'll also see him attacking men he sees as beneath him, while being subservient to men he sees as being superior. He doesn't tend to notice that he's doing this, or that it's strange or problematic.

These men are usually pretty easy to spot, because they'll be the ones laughing at women, staring at their breasts or joking with male friends about how stupid or hot certain women are.

However, some Misogynists have also learned that they can't get away with this as much as they used to. Perhaps they've been disciplined at work or perhaps somebody has challenged their behaviour in the past. These men will still be actively hostile towards women, but they'll try to hide it (and they'll often feel a lot of resentment that they have to hide it). Only when they're in a 'safe place' (amongst other Misogynists, at home or online) will they let their beliefs show.

If a woman inconveniences him, he will be emotionally triggered and will attack her. The levels here vary: some Misogynists will verbally (or even physically) attack a woman if she annoys him, but others need more adversity before they're triggered. All Misogynists have a threshold of annoyance, a line that women must not cross. If she does, he'll use whatever tools he has to 'put her in her place'. He might insult or attack her directly, or try to stir up trouble against her with other people, or try to use procedures at work to get her into trouble. He feels personally wronged, insulted, that she crossed the line. She must be punished.

He believes that he is entitled to certain treatment from women. Again, the levels here vary. Some men believe that a woman should always smile at him, be sexually available and make him feel good about himself. Other men believe that a girlfriend should clean his home, or compliment him regularly to reinforce his self-esteem. Whatever his expectations, they're unconscious. He would take a while to explain to you exactly what he expects women to do for him. These beliefs are firmly held, though. Women who fail to meet his standards as enablers, servants or cheerleaders will make him feel annoyed and probably trigger his hostility.

Sadly, many women have been raised by Misogynists and they will spend their lives unconsciously trying to meet misogynistic standards, to please men or at least not to trigger their hostility. Many women instinctively know that if they annoy a man, or fail to meet his standards, he will attack her (physically or verbally).

If you aren't sure if a man is a Misogynist, watch him in situations where a woman annoys him, inconveniences him, challenges him or outperforms him. If he begins to fall back on degrading or humiliating language, if he tries to undermine her reputation or if he gets overtly hostile towards her, you're probably dealing with a Misogynist.

Misogynists often have strange relationships with their mothers. They will either hate their mothers and bad mouth them a lot, or they will revere and adore their mother as the archetype that all other women should attain.

Misogynists aren't necessarily straight. There are a lot of gay misogynists in the world.

THE RED FLAGS

- Insulting women openly, using degrading or humiliating language (calling women bitches, sluts, mad, dumb...)

- Getting emotionally triggered if a woman ever insults him, corrects him or outperforms him

- Getting emotionally triggered if a woman fails to meet his standards, usually when she doesn't fulfil 'traditional' roles

- Leering at women openly, either alone or when he's with his friends

- Making comments that imply that women are inferior to men

- Hinting that women 'deserved it' if they're ever hurt or abused

- Weird relationship with mother: either hostile or reverential

WHY ARE THESE MEN DANGEROUS TO WOMEN?

A Misogynist will oppress or attack women simply for being women, or given the slightest provocation.

He's dangerous most obviously because he is a physical and psychological threat to women. If a woman triggers him or crosses his threshold, he will feel compelled to attack her in some way. These men are everywhere, and they ruin women's lives.

Misogynists are responsible for:

- A great deal of domestic violence and the high rates of murder of women by their partners

- Most hostile trolling towards women online

- Women being passed over for promotion, or being offered lower salaries than their male counterparts

- Perpetuating ridiculous, harmful stereotypes about women (for example, women are crazy / women can't drive / women are more suited to 'caring' roles than men)

- Supporting anti-women or anti-feminist speakers and groups

- Daughters being conditioned to fear men or to act in pleasing or obliging ways around them

- Sons being conditioned to become Misogynists themselves

A woman will never be safe around a Misogynist. If she conforms to all his expectations, he probably won't attack her. If she never annoys him, he probably won't attack her. But even if she is lucky enough to avoid his physical or psychological abuse, she will always have to walk on eggshells.

WHAT'S THE UNDERLYING PSYCHOLOGY?

A Misogynist is a man who has swallowed patriarchal beliefs hook, line and sinker. A misogynist is a deeply wounded man who doesn't notice or understand the depth of his psychological wounding. He is a living manifestation of the phrase 'hurt people, hurt people'.

He exists in a profound state of isolation, loneliness, emotional incompetence and deep insecurity. He is a very fragile person. He was probably raised and educated to live in a way that fails to meet his core emotional needs, and these unsatisfied needs bring him a lot of psychological pain. He's only willing to identify or acknowledge emotional needs that he sees as 'masculine', which means all his other emotional needs go unsatisfied. This means he will rarely be able to express himself in a vulnerable and healthy way, or take active steps to meet his own emotional needs, and so he spends his life in a state of anxious need. Unable to recognise that his own beliefs are the cause, he looks outside himself for the reasons he isn't happy, fulfilled, relaxed and at ease.

He has no idea that any of this is true, and so he blames all of his behaviour on the world around him, primarily on women. His father and other men around him probably felt the same, and since they blamed women, he has learned to blame women.

A man who isn't able to identify his own emotions and actively regulate them, or to seek help to heal emotional problems, or to change his lifestyle so that his needs get met, is a fragile person. He tends to want to be 'strong', but this word is warped by patriarchy to mean 'isolated', 'emotionless' or 'aggressive'. He will constantly be assessing whether he is good enough or whether he's failing. If he encounters beliefs or products that make him feel stronger, he is very impressionable. He can be easily manipulated or convinced to do things that feed into his beliefs and needs. If you see adverts for cars aimed at men they tend to pander to a man's insecurities and needs to be 'strong'.

He is trapped in a cycle:

- His emotional needs go unnoticed, so he never learns to express himself or regulate his emotions. He's uncomfortable with any feelings that he's been taught are 'unmasculine'. Instead of looking inwards and recognising his failings, then seeking help, he looks outside and expects the world to be different.

- This inability to regulate emotions leads to inherent insecurity. He knows, unconsciously, that he can't handle certain situations.

- He feels bad and unsatisfied by life.

- He's been given a belief structure by his childhood that tells him that women are to blame for all his bad feelings.

- Women trigger him by failing to act in the way he's been taught they should act.

- His feelings reinforce the patriarchal beliefs he was taught as a child.

His core beliefs are:

1. That men are superior to women, or even that women aren't real people at all.

2. 'Traditional' gender roles (those invented during the 19th century). Very simply, this is the idea of 'strong' (meaning isolated) men and subservient women.

3. That women exist to serve men. Women should either provide for him practically, or sexually, or they should reinforce his self-esteem.

4. A view of life as a race or competition.

5. Men are supposed to be 'strong', and men who ask for help are weak.

He's not interested in women as people, women are at best accessories to his lifestyle and at worst, simply objects.

We can split misogynists into two groups:

1. Conscious Misogynists. These guys are becoming more rare, thankfully, but there are still plenty of them around and they tend to inspire Unconscious Misogynists.

   These are men who have actually stopped to think about what they believe, they've reflected on their beliefs and they've consciously decided that they like their hostile views about women. They usually spend their time in echo chambers, either living in remote places where men aren't challenged often, or hanging out online in pro-misogyny, anti-feminist places.

   There is no proper, intellectual basis for misogyny, and you have to be fairly stupid or uneducated to continue believing it when you stop to think about it, but if you aren't ever really challenged then it's possible to think that misogyny is smart, true and valid as an approach to life.

   These men lead the charge against feminism. They will have phrases and slogans, they will chat to other Misogynists to reinforce their beliefs and they will go out of their way to convert other men. Their threshold for attacking women is very low, often simply attacking a woman for existing, or failing to smile at him, or saying the wrong words.

2. Unconscious Misogynists. These are the bulk of Misogynists. These men don't realise they're Misogynists, and would probably be surprised to be called one. They move through their lives without understanding that they are emotionally insecure, and they don't reflect on their strange hostility towards women. They don't see the patterns (which is often obvious to others) around the things that trigger their anger, or make them attack women. They are afraid of psychotherapy, or things like therapy, but don't notice that they are.

   These men are usually educated as children to be hostile towards women by fathers who also felt unsatisfied emotional needs but lacked the skills to identify and deal with them. However, they are also easily manipulated by Conscious Misogynists.

These men, then, have two core problems that lead to all their instability and violence:

1. Emotional ignorance. They don't really notice their own feelings, don't understand how emotions work and can't voice their emotional needs. They tend to actively work to maintain their own ignorance.

2. Embracing a toxic series of beliefs, because these beliefs explain their emotional experience of life. These beliefs have to be taught to a man (or a woman) by somebody

else; nobody naturally comes to believe in patriarchy. They are either taught in early life or by Conscious Misogynists later in life.

WHAT WOULD HEAL THESE MEN?

Misogynists can have all sorts of complicated mental and emotional issues, and they might have a complex web of beliefs about the world, but everything is based on one foundational belief: women are less important, less competent and less human than men. Without this underlying belief, all the rest falls apart.

People who hold these kinds of hostile, othering core beliefs tend to have difficult backgrounds. If you grow up feeling safe, cared-for, listened-to and respected, you tend to develop a strong sense of empathy and a willingness to learn about others. So we're talking here about men who were abandoned, neglected or otherwise failed by their parents and care-givers. As boys, they weren't supported to develop healthy empathy and compassionate beliefs.

If these men can develop a good working relationship with a therapist, they can examine these beliefs, heal the emotional wounds that reinforce it, and understand that their whole world-view is ridiculous. The tricky part, of course, is that the very childhoods that allow misogynistic beliefs to flourish also tends to create cynical, untrusting men. Trust is the foundation of a therapeutic relationship.

In the meantime, these men need to be stopped from causing harm. So the stages in their healing might look like:

1. Being regularly challenged in their behaviour, so they come to realise that there's something wrong with their attitude and beliefs

2. Being reminded that therapy is an option, and supported (ideally by other men) to seek out a therapist they can feel safe with

3. Starting to reflect on their childhoods and understand why they hold such hostility towards women

WHY ARE WOMEN ATTRACTED TO THESE MEN?

It's normal

In so many places, this is just how men act. Women are used to it, men accept it, so if you're a woman who's attracted to men, you just learn to ignore it. So many women have boyfriends or husbands who are Misogynists, and they've just learned to lower their expectations. "Sure, he treats me badly sometimes or talks down to me, but that's just how men are. It's better than being alone."

It's how they expect men to act

If you grow up watching men being dismissive or mean to women, you'll associate that behaviour with manliness, with sexiness or even with safety. At first, a man who treats you with respect or consideration might seem weird, weak or repulsive. This is internalised patriarchy at work. You have been programmed to see disrespect as a good thing.

These men often succeed

In a lot of workplaces, patriarchy still rules supreme. Men who have internalised patriarchy will automatically respect a man who treats women badly, and so those men might get promotions or opportunities that more decent men won't. Laughing at women, telling stories about treating women badly or talking over women in meetings will seem, to these people, like a mark of strength and prestige. So Misogynists who work in these places can earn well, succeed, show off their wealth and seem like a great person to build a family with. A woman who is looking for financial security for her future, and is willing to put up with crappy behaviour, degradation and neglect, will be very happy to get together with these men.

Type 2: User

A User is a man who is only interested in women for their usefulness to him, and he's willing to lie, manipulate or pressure a woman to provide for him.

For many men, this means sex. He'll routinely be on dating apps or picking up women in bars, and he'll have moves and pickup lines to get a woman into bed quickly. He's happy to lie to them or manipulate them into bed, even promising them love or a committed relationship.

Other situations where you can spot Users might include:

- A man who keeps financial control of his wife so she'll look after his children and provide him with other free services of all kinds.

- A man who pursues a second relationship even when he's in a first relationship, so he can end the old connection and immediately move into the new one.

- A man who surrounds himself with attractive women, or dates many women at once, because this makes him look good to other men.

- A male boss who keeps a woman in a low-paid job, promising her a promotion eventually, because it's useful to him that she stays in that job.

- A man who depends on a woman for emotional support and care, and so he manipulates her so she won't leave.

Many of these situations can exist consciously and ethically: a man can be open about his intentions and if he does that, he's not a User because he's showing respect for the woman involved, and she has free choice whether or not she wants to be involved.

Users only see women as accessories. They tend to also see women as 'other', that is they see women as a different type of human being to themselves. To a User, the ethical rules for how you treat men and women are different. This can be similar to Misogynists, who see women as inferior or targets for attack, but Users aren't overtly hostile towards women. They simply see them as useful.

A User can be quite kind and friendly towards women in his life... until they cease to be useful to him. Then he'll lose interest, or manipulate, pressure or force them back into the behaviour he expects.

Users are incapable of genuine friendships with women. He cannot be open, real, vulnerable or emotionally transparent with a woman. He doesn't see the value in a woman beyond the services she provides to him. He wouldn't want to be and he'll lack the skills at doing so.

Some Users do this consciously, intentionally mapping out how they will control women or trick them into doing what he wants them to do. Other Users do this unconsciously, they don't realise that they treat women without respect and don't identify their behaviour as unethical or problematic. Some Users might even be hurt if you confront them and explain that they're a User. Human beings are quite capable of holding conflicting beliefs, so a man can fully believe he's a good guy who behaves decently, and not notice he also uses women without respect or regard.

THE RED FLAGS

Telltale behaviour of a User might be:

- He's very smooth and practised at picking up women
- He says things that suggest he doesn't have respect for women
- He boasts to his male friends that he can get what he wants from women, or from a specific woman
- He talks about his power and status a lot
- He hangs out with other User men, who condone and support his behaviour
- He will tend to talk about women's appearance a lot
- He speaks as if women are 'the enemy' who must be controlled or disarmed

WHY ARE THESE MEN DANGEROUS TO WOMEN?

Some women play along with Users, that's pretty common. Some women marry Users completely consciously, knowing that they, too, intend to work this situation to their advantage. She will use him for his wealth and status and she will let him use her for her beauty and potential as a mother - she doesn't care that she'll never have a close relationship with him. Other women sleep with Users because they, too, just want sex and they see his bullshit pickup lines and promises for what they are. Some women use men just as Users are using them.

The main risk of being involved with a User is not knowing they're a User. These guys will never really respect a woman or connect with her in a genuine, real, vulnerable way. He doesn't know how and he doesn't see the point (unless that's the thing he's using her for).

Users don't tend to be dangerous in the way Misogynists are: they aren't usually a physical threat and they're less likely to be mocking or degrading. The danger in Users is when a woman doesn't really appreciate what's happening. She might not see through his lies, or she might convince herself that she can change him or win him over. She can't. She isn't a full person to him. She is an object which exists to provide for him.

Users can hurt women emotionally, they can ruin their careers, they can trap a woman in difficult situations or they can manipulate women and destroy their self-esteem and confidence. So the dangers of a User are psychological, but these mental and emotional wounds can then affect a woman's life in profound ways.

WHAT'S THE UNDERLYING PSYCHOLOGY?

Unlike the Misogynist, a User isn't actively hostile to women, he just isn't interested in their needs as human beings. Women are objects to provide for him, rather than complex and interesting people in their own rights. Some Users treat men in just the same way (things to satisfy his needs at work, or for entertainment, or to look good) while others might have proper, rich relationships with men but not with women.

So there's something missing in the way he sees the world and the way he forms connections with people. The missing piece is this: a genuine interest and curiosity in other people, specifically in women. He just isn't interested. Maybe he'll ask questions as part of his seduction routine, but he doesn't really care.

Healthy, well-adjusted people are interested in other people. Human beings are social animals, so forming connections with other people is something we instinctively crave. To do that, we need to understand people so we tend to be curious about people, to be interested, to want to know what makes a person tick. The deeper the connection we want, the more we tend to ask questions, watch the way they do things, or find other ways to learn about them. What makes them happy? What do they want from life? What are their interests and passions? Where did they come from and where are they going? What do they know and what do they believe? What's it like to be them, and how do they see the world?

Some people do this learning consciously, some people don't realise they're doing it, but the driver is always the same: we're genuinely curious about other people.

In the User, something has gone wrong here. His response to be curious about a woman's humanity isn't there. She is just a vessel to fulfil his needs. Perhaps he was never taught how to connect with other people when he was young, or perhaps he's been through some traumatic event that taught him to be hyper-independent. There are psychological disorders which stop people being interested in the humanity of others (psychopaths, sociopaths or particularly profound forms of narcissism), and a man with these conditions is probably not going to develop deeper interests in how people feel. A few Users might have these conditions, but not all of them. Most men can heal enough to remember how to see women as complex, interesting human beings.

WHAT WOULD HEAL THESE MEN?

Assuming a User doesn't have a personality disorder, his healing just means learning that women are real people, and that it's a good thing to focus on their feelings and needs.

Exposure to feminist thought can be very helpful. A User just doesn't realise or care that women have complex internal worlds, so reading, watching or listening to feminist material can force him to consider things that he doesn't normally think about. It might challenge his behaviour, or make him reconsider his beliefs, or help him feel the impacts of his actions and become more empathetic.

He will probably need therapy. If we assume that most people have this instinct to be interested in others, then something must have got stuck or interrupted in a User. He might need time with a professional to examine his childhood and teenage years to understand what happened to 'switch off' his instinct to be interested in the humanity of women.

WHY ARE WOMEN ATTRACTED TO THESE MEN?

Some women are happy to use men while they're used in return. As long as this is conscious and as long as she's also protecting and caring for herself, this is fine. However, if you spend too long with someone who just isn't interested in who you are as a person, it may begin to impact your self-esteem and emotional wellbeing.

Many women will find time with a User confusing, hurtful and dehumanising.

A User will know how to manipulate a woman into finding them attractive or appealing. It's something they've spent years perfecting. They will have techniques, or lines, or even ways to force a woman into sex, or a relationship, or marriage.

So if you're a woman dating a man, it's important to be aware if he's a User. Try to work out if he's genuinely interested in who you are: does he seem to care about your feelings and needs? Does he ask questions that don't serve him? Is he just doing and saying things to get what he needs from you, or is there a real connection here?

Type 3: Timebomb

Almost all men in our culture grow up being taught patriarchal values by their parents, their friends or the entertainment they watch. It could be subtle things like being taught that women are more emotional than men, but often it's much more than that. They can be taught to sexualise women and see them purely as sexual objects, or they can believe that women are 'other' and lesser than men, or they can be taught to compartmentalise women into certain limited roles, like mothers, pure virgins or sluts, which denies the genuine and complex personalities and needs of women. Men are drip-fed these ideas throughout their lives.

One thing that tends to lurk behind all the things men are taught is the idea of entitlement, which I talked about earlier in this book. Men can be taught that they are entitled to women's respect, their admiration, their care, perhaps their subservience. Men can be taught they are entitled to be revered as strong, as leaders, as powerful and masculine. Men can also feel they are entitled to success, wealth, power or influence. It's part of the reason men tend to be more comfortable applying for jobs that are a big leap forward, where they don't meet all the requirements in the job description. They have this unconscious belief that they're entitled to high pay and success, and they ride this sense of entitlement into job interviews. It contributes to how many men are in senior positions: they're more willing to risk things because something is whispering to them that they deserve to be there.

This isn't the same as earning respect and social position, it's the idea that a man should receive it simply for being a man. If a man has worked hard, or done exceptional things, or been a steadfast friend or partner then sure, he's earned respect. We're not talking about that. Entitlement is the idea that a man doesn't need to do anything to deserve respect and status, especially from women. He should just receive it, magically, because that's how the world is meant to work. Women are meant to make him feel good about himself.

Some men continue to actively believe this and act like it's literally true, and they tend to be Misogynists and they're usually obvious.

Many more men hold this idea on a more subtle, unconscious level, and this is pretty common and widespread. Men can be otherwise good, self-aware, respectful, fair people but if they aren't getting the things they feel they're entitled to, they will feel like something is wrong. It's up to each man to recognise what's happening inside himself, and to understand when he's being motivated or driven by toxic unconscious programming. Many men manage this, but some don't.

These are the Timebombs. A Timebomb is a nice guy most of the time, he's someone you want to spend time with and he might be very attractive. However, somewhere inside him there are emotional triggers. Perhaps it's just a certain level of stress and pressure in his life, or perhaps it's certain experiences or words. Humiliation or embarrassment will tend to be strong triggers because they're the exact opposite of what patriarchy teaches a man he's entitled to.

Many people get upset when they're stressed or triggered, but Timebombs explode into rage. As you get to know them, you'll know the signs. Perhaps they go really quiet, or perhaps they try to leave situations before they explode. Perhaps you notice physical signs, like wringing his hands or fidgeting or going red in the face. What's coming is an outburst of unconstrained anger and fury. In extreme cases this can become physical violence.

Spending time with a Timebomb can feel like you're always walking on thin ice. You learn that there are things you can't say or things you can't do, because it'll trigger them. You learn to watch out for the warning signs. People in long-term relationships with Timebombs might learn to structure everything around their emotionally erratic partner. Days are structured to remove his triggers. Certain topics aren't discussed. Holidays are arranged to avoid anything that might set him off.

Other Timebombs are more unpredictable and you never know what's going to set them off. You'll be having a relationship with one person, when suddenly he flips to being another person.

Yet other Timebombs cannot allow themselves to channel their huge emotional outbursts into direct rage. They might have other early-life training, like an abusive father or something else that strongly conditioned them to never explode. These are still Timebombs, you'll still see the sudden switch of personality and the surge of anger inside them, but they will express it in other ways. They'll break things, or shout at the telly, or hurt themselves, or say mean or cruel things over a longer period of time to try to dissipate their intense emotions.

Of course people like this exist across all genders. Some people simply aren't very good at managing uncomfortable emotions and they bottle them up until they explode. But there is something unique about how this happens in men. A Timebombs is carrying this subtle, unconscious belief that the world (and especially women) should treat him in certain ways, so if that's not happening it begins to build pressure inside him. His sense of entitlement feeds into his other frustrations, and he is particularly vulnerable to emotional triggers that conflict with the things he feels he's entitled to.

THE RED FLAGS

- He gets suddenly angry for no apparent reason

- He seems has two personalities: a stable guy and an angry guy

- People learn to avoid saying or doing things around him in case they 'set him off'

- He sometimes says mean or degrading things about women that you wouldn't normally expect him to say

- He is very sensitive to embarrassment, humiliation or ridicule

WHAT'S THE UNDERLYING PSYCHOLOGY?

The psychology of a Timebomb is based on internalised patriarchy, which I've talked about a lot in this book, but these men are also doing their best (with the limited tools they've learned so far) to repress and control their outrage and anger. The world isn't providing them with the things that they were taught to expect, and this makes them angry, but this is usually a completely unconscious process. They don't know why they're angry, or why certain situations trigger them so strongly, but they do know that anger isn't safe or welcome so they learn to squash it down.

Anger is not a 'bad' emotion. Like all feelings, anger has things to teach us and it's an essential part of our emotional makeup. But in the same way that patriarchy isn't normally something we're taught about as children, we aren't taught how to handle our emotions. Most people just go through life trying to be happy, trying to seem happy, and trying to avoid or repress their 'negative emotions'.

Timebombs want to feel in control, like all people do. They want to believe they're good people. They are probably as confused and scared by their anger as everyone around them, and so they will fight (again, usually unconsciously) to stay in control.

This creates a pressure-cooker situation. Emotions that are repressed or ignored will tend to become more intense until they get the attention they need. It's up to all of us to learn how emotions work so we can develop a healthy relationship with them, but a

Timebomb hasn't done this learning. His experience of life conflicts with his beliefs about his male entitlement, and this makes him angry, and he doesn't know how to either confront his beliefs or safely deal with the anger.

His lack of skills and awareness make him prone to explode.

WHY ARE THESE MEN DANGEROUS?

Sometimes these men are literally, physically, dangerous. The high rate of murders of women by their partners can be explained in part, I think, by the Timebomb personality type. Timebombs who get physical in their anger and outrage are not safe to be around.

However, Timebombs who aren't violent are also dangerous to be around. They can be frightening to live with, or his partner can feel their 'walking on eggshells' a lot of the time, for fear of triggering an outburst. If you live with a Timebomb, you will know it. There will be things you avoid doing or saying because you don't want to trigger his anger, and over time this can affect your personality and confidence.

WHAT WOULD HEAL THESE MEN?

Men with internalised patriarchy (which is almost all men) need healing and they need to let go of their toxic beliefs about the roles of women and men. Often this means they need to be challenged, ideally by other men.

Timebombs are men who try to keep their patriarchal beliefs and impulses in check, but these beliefs still lurk inside them, influencing their expectations for how the world should be. They must go deeper into themselves to confront and surrender these beliefs, so they become safe to be around. Simply squashing your feelings and ideas down isn't enough. I guess you could say that it's a noble beginning: these men are doing their best to stop their toxic programming from hurting people. However, as long as they're still secretly carrying patriarchal views, they're a ticking Timebomb.

These men need exposure to feminist thought and to progressive men who have walked the same path and learned how to be better. They also need to properly understand their own emotions and learn how to process their anger in a healthy way. I'd encourage these men to challenge themselves deeply to go looking for ways to learn and heal.

Therapy is, of course, also helpful for these men, to be sure that the change is real and deep and lasting.

WHY ARE WOMEN ATTRACTED TO THESE MEN?

If a woman is attracted to a Timebomb because she hasn't seen his anger yet, that's just an honest mistake. A Timebomb can be a wonderful, attractive, fun, warm person most of the time. The fact that he is generally repressing his anger can also make him seem like a kind and thoughtful person.

However, if you know that he's a Timebomb and you continue to find him appealing and attractive, then you need to explore your own internalised patriarchy. You may have unconscious beliefs about the roles of women and men which will put you in danger of tolerating bad behaviour from your partner.

Type 4: Stone

As a coach, my client base is always pretty balanced between women and men. People from all sorts of backgrounds hire me, but I go into first sessions with some information about who they are and what they want. By the time someone sits in the chair for the first time, or logs on to their first coaching call, they've already spoken to me and they've completed a form telling me about themselves and their goals.

I do need to make some assumptions, though. When I'm coaching a man, I assume that, amongst anything else he wants to achieve, he's going to need to work on his emotions. Men just don't usually get the same kind of emotional education that women get.

This means there are lots of men out there who don't understand their feelings, don't notice what they're feeling, ignore their erratic behaviour and dismiss 'emotional' people as stupid. I'm calling this group of men: Stones.

A Stone man is one who is totally matter-of-fact about everything. He only focuses on practical things: his job, his to-do list, the things that people expect of him. This is the only defining trait of Stones: he can be a good man or a bad man, he can act respectfully or not, he can be effective or successful or he can fail at all the important things in his life. You will find Stones in all areas of life.

Not understanding emotions is like lacking another essential faculty, like sight or hearing. However, if you can't see or hear then you know that you're lacking something that other people have. You recognise that you're the odd one out, and you do things to compensate for your loss. The difference with Stone men is that emotional incompetence in men is so common that our culture actually supports and enables it, masking it from men and letting them believe that the problem is other people.

The trope of highly emotional, crazy women is really common and you'll hear both men and women making jokes about it. Meanwhile, emotionless men are celebrated. So, a man who lacks skills and competence with his emotions is given a lot of help to mask his inadequacies. These are men with profound skill gaps in areas that are essential for meaningful relationships and a proper enjoyment of life, and yet our society makes it so easy for him to tell himself that he's the sane one.

A Stone can go his entire life without anyone convincing him that he's the problem. Until someone can get through to him, he will continue to make the same mistakes.

A Stone man doesn't notice his own feelings, unless they are 'masculine' feelings like anger, competitiveness or ambition around his career or masculine hobbies.

He will regularly make choices based on things like fear, insecurity, longing, emotional overwhelm, delight, the need to be loved or the need to feel safe, but he won't notice that he has those feelings and so he won't understand his true motives. When people don't understand the choices they make, they tend to make up stories to explain their own behaviour. People don't like to feel out of control. It's really common for most people to invent explanations for their behaviour because they can't or won't see the true reasons. Most of us do it, fairly often, without noticing that we've done it. For Stone men, this is a way of life. They make choices that are motivated by emotion, but they'll either ignore their actions altogether, or they will tell themselves stories that fill in the gaps.

An example of this is when they get upset. Let's imagine a Stone man is at work and his company announces that they are down-sizing and some people will be losing their jobs. Some people in his team will be fired. He's scared, and he's anxious that other people will outperform him, and he's trying to keep focused on his work despite his fear, insecurity and emotional overwhelm. He gets snappy, he stops hanging out with his work buddies as much, he starts falling out with his wife.

The Stone man can't understand what he's feeling. He notices that things are changing around him, but he doesn't notice that he's the cause. As his anxiety increases, he notices the fights at work, the fact his friends seem more distant and all the conflict at home. Why, he asks himself, are these people being so weird? They must be emotional, which means they're incapable of being mature, logical and disciplined. He ignores his own part in things and blames other people. The more emotional they seem to him, the easier he can blame them.

'Emotional' people, to him, are those who cry, or get visibly upset, or talk about their feelings, or people who take steps to care for themselves or set conscious boundaries. All of these things are, to a Stone man, evidence of immaturity, weakness or stupidity.

Stone men are very poor at empathy. Empathy is a fairly advanced emotional skill: it's the ability to be emotionally sensitive and receptive towards another person and put yourself in their shoes, feeling what they feel. Stone men refuse to acknowledge the importance of emotions at all, so empathy is beyond them. Due to this, they are often slow to empathise with people who are suffering, and the further away they are, the more difficult he finds it. He will usually need other people to convince him that he should care.

This 'distance' can be physical (seeing people suffering in another country) or it might be people who are different to him. Stone men can easily become prejudiced or uncaring towards minority groups, women, or people of a different sexual orientation. They are 'other', they are alien to him, and he lacks the skill at empathising with them.

Telltale signs of Stone men include:

- Joking about crazy emotional women
- Mocking people who show 'non-masculine' emotions
- Always seeming logical and in-control
- Not understanding when people explain their feelings
- Mocking or attacking people who are different from them, for example minority groups
- Doing things that seem very emotional, but denying that he felt anything, and making up a non-emotional reason why he did it
- Trying to convince or pressure other people into being less emotional

WHY ARE THESE MEN DANGEROUS TO WOMEN?

Stone men pose two main dangers to women:

They can become threatening if they're emotionally triggered

Stone men don't understand their own feelings, which means they can't develop skills and emotional regulation. In well-balanced people, emotional regulation means noticing what you're feeling (either feeling it directly or figuring it out based on what your body is doing), then knowing what it's *not* ok to do (blaming others, lashing out, being passive-aggressive) and instead having well-developed, healthy habits for dealing with your feelings.

This whole mechanism doesn't exist in Stone men, and our society shelters them from needing to face this fact. This means that, when they are emotionally triggered, they are effectively young children in big, strong bodies. So imagine a toddler, having a tantrum, but tall, strong and fully capable of doing and saying hurtful things.

This doesn't necessarily mean he's violent (though in extreme cases you need to watch out for this). His behaviour might instead be:

- Sulking
- Blaming and persecuting
- Withdrawing love and affection
- Breaking things
- Passive-aggressive behaviour
- Physically leaving or just 'checking out'
- Punishing in petty ways
- Judging and blaming others

They can be erode your self-esteem

To him, he's the sane one while emotional people (which usually includes all women) are crazy. This means he will tend to progressively undermine women over time, mocking them or criticising them for their behaviour. If you're romantically involved with a Stone man, this can be a crappy experience that will lower your self-esteem over time. He has one narrative: that you're difficult and annoying, and he will express this whenever he is emotionally triggered. You will always be the problem, you are the one at fault all the time, and he will remember examples of times you were stupid and emotional.

Some women can endure this without being undermined, but it takes a great deal of personal strength and a clear understanding that emotions are an essential part of the human experience. If you have any insecurities, or if you want to date someone who cherishes your emotional skills, don't date a Stone man.

WHAT'S THE UNDERLYING PSYCHOLOGY?

Almost all human beings have the full range of emotions. The number of people who are unable to feel emotions at all is very small. Sure, there are some psychological conditions that make it harder for people to notice or access their feelings but, again, the number of people with these conditions isn't very large.

Studies have shown that parents or teachers tend to provide a lot more emotional education to girls than to boys. When talking to girls, they will say things like "you must love that, your whole face lights up", or "did he upset you?", or "why are you so angry?". This becomes a whole education for girls which boys don't tend to get. Girls learn that when they're feeling something inside, there's a name for it, and they learn to connect the physical sensation with the emotion. They're taught what other people see when they're feeling that emotion, and they learn different ways to act, and they're taught which responses are welcome and which ones upset or annoy other people. This process can cause its own problems if a young girl is taught, for example, that it's not ok to express anger, but she's still getting an education in the way emotions work. By the time most girls mature into women, they are able to identify and name their feelings, even if they don't know they have these skills.

Meanwhile, parents and teachers are less likely to talk to boys about feelings, instead focusing on practical things. Boys are encouraged to be physical, and even when they get upset, people are more likely to do things for them to cheer them up than to help them understand why they're upset or what to do about it.

People tend to say that girls mature faster than boys, and people tend to believe that women are more emotional than men. There might be lots of reasons for this, but surely this is one of them. Women have been taught to recognize their feelings, to understand how their actions and their feelings are linked, and which ways of expressing their feelings are acceptable.

Also, so much of our education is based on what we witness, rather than what we're taught. Boys often see their fathers being unemotional, or mocking people who display emotions. Other boys see their fathers as weak or unstable, and they grow up determined not to be like that.

A minority of boys are taught how to understand and express their feelings, and some teach themselves as they get older. That's why fewer men are Stones now than in older generations: our education is better.

Stones are men who lack essential life skills, usually because of an impoverished or even abusive childhood, but they are able to hide from this fact because society understands and expects emotionless men. A Stone is able to tell himself that he's strong and independent, when really he is a victim of a poor upbringing and of a society that empowers emotionally incompetent men.

There are a lot of Stone men in positions of power, for example senior roles in companies, corporations or in government. They can't empathise, they can't make decisions based on compassion or intuition, they can't feel their own responses to things, they are hamstrung and limited and wounded…but they can live their whole lives being successful and wealthy and being told that they're great men.

These men *can* learn how to do better. They can break into a new way of understanding the world, they can learn how they really work and they can develop the skills to emotionally regulate and empathise. It does happen. Stone men hire me all the time and, when they finish their work with me, they're having happier relationships, they're better leaders and they have richer and more stable emotional lives (including more happiness).

It's just a shame that there is so much protection for Stone men that stops them from ever confronting their flaws.

WHAT WOULD HEAL THESE MEN?

These men need an education in how emotions work, and they need to learn the skills to notice, correctly identify and process their own feelings. This is a lot of learning to do, but it's absolutely possible. There are books and other resources to teach these skills - I even have a blog article on my website about developing emotional mastery.

The tricky bit with a Stone man is to convince them that this is a good idea.

The first steps in learning about feelings are noticing what's happening in your body and what subtle sensations you can pick up in different situations. Your emotions are always there, always flowing inside you, so first we need to begin to notice what they're doing and what they're telling us. This can be destabilising and weird at first. Someone who's doing mental and emotional development will often become more vulnerable and feel less in-control than before they started. They're noticing all these new feelings and they're coming to understand themselves in a whole new way. This can be scary. Eventually we integrate all the things we're learning and we become a wiser, more aware, stronger person…but there's no shortcut. We have to do the work, and go through the struggle.

Stone men know this, or at least they know that beginning to connect with their feelings is going to leave them more vulnerable. We can see, then, that a man who doesn't notice his own feelings is deeply afraid of himself and what he might find if he begins to look inside.

My clients, or people I meet in the world, often say to me "people never change". I say to them "I agree, most people will avoid changing, but people are often changed by the world". Most of us will stick with one way of doing things for our whole lives, until it becomes really obvious to us that it doesn't work, or that there's a better way. We use the most ridiculous or ineffective strategies to solve problems in our lives until something forces us to reconsider them. This often comes in the shape of a crisis: losing a job, the end of a precious relationship or a health scare. Occasionally it takes the shape of someone challenging us so strongly that we're finally willing to consider long-held beliefs or habits. Something has to matter so much to us or shake us so badly that we're willing to try something new.

Stone men stubbornly refuse to learn about their humanity until life forces them to. If they're lucky, they will meet someone who can show them that emotional competence would dramatically improve their lives. More often, they will need a significant personal crisis before they're willing to consider changing and growing.

WHY ARE WOMEN ATTRACTED TO THESE MEN?

Stone men are extremely consistent, and they tend to display a lot of the traditional markers of patriarchal success. They might be competitive, aggressive, confident or have strong tribal affiliations (for example to a sports team, a brand, a town or a political party).

Some of these qualities can be very attractive on their own. It's sexy for a man to be strong and successful in his chosen field. However, if a woman carries her own internalised patriarchy she will see emotionless men as strong and successful and she'll be drawn to them.

The risk of dating or marrying one, however, is that you condemn yourself to a life of patriarchal standards. He won't be able to meet you on an emotional level and he'll never understand you. He will tend to protect himself from having to confront his own feelings by mocking or belittling you for having emotions.

Type 5: Butterfly

Forming and maintaining strong connections with other people is central to being human. We're social animals. Countless studies have shown that it's the relationships we build that, ultimately, matter most to us, and people who have been interviewed at the end of life, and asked about their biggest regrets, often say that they wish they'd made more time for the people they love.

Despite this, it takes a lot of skill to navigate relationships. We need to know how to find the kinds of people we like, we need the self-belief to approach people, we need to be good at building bridges with them, we need to communicate effectively and we need the resilience to handle the inevitable ups and downs of relating to other people.

Some men simply don't try. They aren't interested in it, or they don't have the skills, or things in their past have taught them not to try.

Like many of the toxic male archetypes that we're examining in this book, our society provides a way for these men to avoid admitting that they have work to do. There's a place for the lone wolf, or the rogue, or the social butterfly. Men can tell themselves that they're fine, even though they don't maintain strong connections and often feel alone.

More specifically, Butterfly men move from person to person, taking what they need, but never forming lasting connections. They might have some friends, but those are either old friendships from earlier chapters of their lives, or they're shallow acquaintances.

If you date Butterfly men, he'll seem engaging at first, he'll seem to be into you, maybe he'll even love bomb you and offer you the world, but he'll lose interest over time until he vanishes. Some Butterfly men will ghost people they're still getting to know, while others will hang around for a while before fading away. The ending will always feel confusing and unsatisfying to the woman he's been dating: she might feel like she's done something wrong, or spend a long time afterwards trying to understand what just happened.

Some Butterflies go through life blaming others for connections going wrong. Each time they lose contact with someone, or decide to leave, or stop putting effort into a connection, they will have a story about what the other person did wrong. They tend not to notice their own role in the breakup.

Other Butterflies know that they are the problem, that they lack some essential skill or ability to form lasting connections, but they don't go looking for solutions. These Butterflies are insecure and react strongly to being questioned or challenged about their behaviour. They come to believe they're simply not destined to find connections that last.

Either way, Butterflies begin new relationships but quickly abandon them and move on to the next.

THE RED FLAGS

- A history of short relationships

- Intense connection really quickly

- Discomfort in making plans or talking about the future

- Talk about commitment makes him uncomfortable

- Ghosting or rapidly fading away

WHAT'S THE UNDERLYING PSYCHOLOGY?

A Butterfly is a man who's very uncomfortable in a long-term relationship. The nature of men like this can vary a lot.

If a man is consciously looking for a good time and fully intends to leave as soon as it stops feeling easy then we're just talking about a specific kind of User. He doesn't empathise with women, he uses them for sex, affection or security.

However, there are a lot of men who really want to fall in love and make a lasting relationship, but still fall into a predictable pattern of disconnecting or leaving. They might not have even noticed they have this pattern, or they might know about it but not understand it. Often, they believe that it's nothing to do with them, they just keep meeting the wrong women. Eventually, they tell themselves, I'll meet someone who's just right and I won't need to shut down, run away or reject them.

They carry on, forming connections with women because they feel passionate or excited or because they see huge potential in this connection, but quickly the passion fades and they feel a need to leave. He might say she's asking too much, or she's making him feel uncomfortable, or she's putting pressure on him. Most often, it just quickly stops "feeling right". He'll feel a need to leave, and he won't usually do it gracefully or compassionately.

Personal development is about understanding yourself. A few people are lucky enough to have childhoods where they get taught about their feelings, about making good choices, about being conscious of what they're doing and why...but this is rare. Most of us just arrive in adulthood feeling totally confused and baffled, but since everyone seems to feel the same, we just try to do our best.

Learning about yourself and healing is about dropping through layers of awareness. At first you notice what you're doing: you begin to notice your patterns of choices and behaviour, even if your own actions seem weird to you, or make you feel uncomfortable. After that, you begin learning about basic psychology: you might speak to a therapist or read some books. If you get into this stuff, you can go very deep into exploring the human condition.

As we learn and grow, our level of consciousness grows. We notice more, we feel more, we make links and understand more. We're present in the moment and conscious of what's going on inside us. The first main goal of personal development is control: we understand ourselves so deeply that we can make empowered, conscious choices instead of random unconscious ones.

Butterflies are men who have avoided this kind of work. They're often scared of what's lurking inside them, so they don't want to look too deeply. Their friends often find them predictable, knowing their patterns really well. If a Butterfly has done any personal development work at all, he always stops before he meets the things that are actually causing the real problems. There will be topics he won't discuss (maybe his relationship with his parents, or his parent's divorce, or how he's never healed from a bad breakup).

To navigate relationships, we all need to balance two core skills: boundaries and vulnerability. We need to set clear boundaries that we communicate well, so both people in the relationship are kept safe, and we need to be willing to open ourselves deeply to the other person, being willing to let them into thoughts and our emotional worlds.

Butterflies cannot navigate these skills. Their boundary-setting tends to be inconsistent and volatile, and they tend to be afraid of vulnerability. Perhaps they manage these things for a short while, but something in their psychology will make it impossible to maintain.

WHY ARE THESE MEN DANGEROUS?

The main danger of a Butterfly is the reckless hurt they cause while they're dating. They will leave a trail of confused, angry, frustrated women as they move through the dating world. Some of these women will just shrug it off and say, well he was an asshole, I won't let that happen again. However, if the relationship had lasted a little while and she was beginning to feel safe and vulnerable with him, it can be shocking to feel suddenly rejected or abandoned.

If you've been through this experience, it's helpful to identify him as a Butterfly. It's so easy to feel like you must be the problem, or you must have done something wrong, or there's something wrong with you. Realising that he's a Butterfly, and he simply doesn't have the awareness or skills to handle a meaningful relationship will help you to shift the focus away from yourself. Maybe there are things for you to learn here, but meeting a man who's just incompetent in relationships isn't your fault.

WHAT WOULD HEAL THESE MEN?

A Butterfly is simply a man who lacks skills, or a man who hasn't healed essential things inside himself.

Obviously, all human beings are complex and every man has a great deal going on inside him, but men who consistently behave like Butterflies are probably just in need of long-term therapy, a lot of time reflecting and learning about himself, and the courage to keep healing even when it gets hard and frightening.

These men don't necessarily have lots of toxic beliefs. Most often, he's just lacking skills and awareness. If he can find those things, he can grow beyond being a Butterfly.

WHY ARE WOMEN ATTRACTED TO THESE MEN?

Like everyone else, Butterflies are doing their best to meet their own needs. He knows he needs companionship, connection and sex, so he's going looking for it. He can often master the skills of meeting, attracting and connecting with a woman, he just can't maintain that connection for very long.

For this reason, Butterflies are often very attractive. They might work on their appearance. They might be suave, seductive or exciting in the way they talk. They might have good ideas for first dates. They might be good in bed.

However, if you don't want to wake up one day and find that the man who's seemed so fun, so sexy and so interesting has just vanished, be sure to look out for the red flags of the Butterfly.

Type 6: Pornosexual

So many adults today grew up watching pornography. The internet makes it free and easy, and parents tend to live in denial about their kids watching porn. It's pretty common now for young kids to be exposed to porn, and it becomes part of young people's education about sex.

Many men regularly watch porn, and porn addiction amongst men is a significant problem for their own mental health. Does porn immediately cause problems for most people? No. In general, I would say that watching porn, either alone or as a couple, isn't always harmful. However, a man who constantly watches porn is at risk of becoming a Pornosexual. These men lose the distinction between performance and reality. They begin to expect themselves to perform like a male porn star, and they begin to expect women to act like the women they see on the screen. They can lose the ability to find non-pornographic sex arousing, which leads to an inability to connect emotionally and can cause performance issues as they aren't getting the stimulation they've grown to expect.

I'll cover the effects that regular porn use can cause in men, but you will know a Pornosexual man by his obsession with the visual experience of sex, by his requests that sex be like the porn he's seen, or by his inability to connect during sex, even though he's able to connect outside of sex.

Common effects of regular porn use on men include:

DISTORTED BELIEFS AND STANDARDS

Men can come to expect all the things they see in porn, both from women and from themselves. They expect women to provide everything they've seen in porn. Women who are using dating apps have told me that many men now expect not only sex on the first date, but also anal sex, fetish-based sex or all sorts of uncomfortable and strange positions *on the first date*. These men have normalised all the things they've seen in porn and now simply expect it to be part of their real sex life.

Pornosexual men can expect the same physical standards from women that they see in porn. In these cases, they're only excited by women who are flawless, who've had breast enlargements, who have blonde hair and who wear makeup. They will swipe through dating apps looking for women who look like porn stars, and they'll judge women who don't conform to these standards.

These men also expect themselves to perform perfectly, to show no emotion or make any sounds during sex, and they expect themselves to never have doubts or insecurities. They can believe that it's a key part of sexual confidence to have a very large penis, and they'll either feel inadequate if they can't measure up, or they'll go looking for gadgets, pills or even surgery to try to solve what they believe is a problem.

In short: these men expect themselves to stop being real, genuine humans while they're having sex and they will judge themselves as failing if they fall part of these artificial standards.

PHYSICAL DESENSITISATION

Pornosexual men will tend to masturbate a lot, which over time can lead to physical desensitisation. This in turn can make real sex unsatisfying or difficult for him.

EMOTIONAL DESENSITISATION

Watching porn is nothing like having sex. There's no connection with another human being, there's no mental or emotional aspect to what's happening, it's a purely visual experience. However, it can feel real. If you think about the times you've been in the cinema watching a movie and you completely lose yourself in the movie, where you're totally immersed and it feels like you're really there… that's how porn can feel if the viewer really immerses themselves in the images on the screen. The separation between the man and the action disappears and he forgets about the fact this is a 2D image being played in front of him.

Over time, this can rewrite his emotional experience of anything sexual. He loses his ability to open up, to feel present. Being with a real woman can feel challenging or weird to these men, and in response they turn the experience of sex into a porn-like experience. They become a voyeur of what's happening, rather than a present, connected person. At this point, they've become emotionally absent and they will just feel like a robot.

Pornosexuals, then, can become emotionally desensitised to anything sexual. They lose normal emotional responses and feel numb, remote or even harsh during sex.

INABILITY TO FORM GENUINE SEXUAL CONNECTIONS

Sex is a complex thing and it has many forms. No matter somebody's gender, or their background, or their emotional range, sex will be different things to them at different times. There's no absolute standard for what sex *should* be. Sometimes it will be just like scratching an itch: you both have a need and having sex will deal with that need. Sometimes it'll be rough and animalistic. Sometimes it can be tender, gentle, with a great deal of eye contact: a deep expression of love and emotional bonding. Sometimes it can be spiritual and transcendent. Sometimes it goes well, sometimes it goes wrong. Sometimes it's funny. Sometimes sex can be psychologically healing, or bring something important to light that you can discuss later. Sometimes people use sex to explore taboo or shadow things that they don't feel allowed to explore in other areas of their lives.

All of these, and many others, are forms that sex can take. All have their time and place and all are normal.

The level of connection you form during sex will also vary, from the wham-bam-thank–you-mam experience to a long, slow and profound joining of hearts and minds. There are times you want to connect deeply with your partner and times that it doesn't really matter that much.

However, if somebody loses the ability to form sexual connections, that becomes a problem.

By sexual connection, I mean the ability to:

- Be fully present and focused on what's happening
- Be emotionally vulnerable and able to empathically sense what your partner is experiencing
- Take active interest in making sure everyone is ok, safe and enjoying themselves
- Be able to take pleasure in your partner experiencing pleasure

This sexual connection might be stronger during some encounters than others, but we all need the ability to do these things, otherwise we miss out on many of the things sex has to offer, and we risk being distant, neglectful or even abusive.

Pornosexuals are men whose primary experience of sex is pornographic, and over time they will tend to lose their skills at forming and maintaining sexual connection. The screen doesn't expect them to connect, it doesn't feel anything and it has no needs. If a video isn't working for a Pornosexual, he can just skip to a new one. At best, his skills at forming genuine connections begin to fade and atrophy. At worst, he loses the ability to distinguish sex from porn and no longer makes any effort to connect. Even if he falls in love and wants to be as close to his partner, he no longer forms sexual connections so sex becomes a problem in his relationship.

SELFISHNESS IN SEX

A pornosexual man can lose the ability to tell real sex apart from watching pornography, which means his partner becomes merely an accessory to his own pleasure. He may be conscious that he's merely using his partner to get himself off, or he may be completely unaware of it. If a man has been using porn since he was young, he may have never developed the ability to experience sex as different from masturbating.

Men with this issue will be selfish lovers, they will insist on their partners looking a certain way, acting in certain ways, or saying certain things, and they'll all feel 'porny'. People can bring all sorts of fantasies to sex and that's fine, so long as they're consciously discussed and everyone consents to them. Sex, however, is two people experiencing something together. A man who is only able to perceive sex as another kind of porn is in need of healing and personal growth, and he can hurt his partner by disregarding her needs or even her identity, instead turning her into an accessory for achieving a selfish kind of sexual fulfilment.

PORN ADDICTION

Addictions are medical problems, where a person loses the ability to control their behaviour around their addiction. Just as an alcoholic can't regulate their drinking, somebody addicted to porn can't stop watching porn. Addicts aren't just enthusiastic about things: they can't stop themselves.

Addictions tend to be things that alter brain chemistry in some way, so this addiction can be physical. However, psychological dependence is also real: a person who has become addicted to an experience or sensation and now they can't stop.

Unsurprisingly, porn addiction is a growing problem in our culture. People seek treatment for it all the time, and while statistics around this are difficult to measure, it might be as high as 5% of all adults regard themselves as addicted to pornography.

If a Pornosexual man has developed an addiction then he won't be able to stop consuming porn. He will need to incorporate it into his sex life, or he'll sneak off to watch it without his partner knowing. This can be as harmful to a relationship as any other addiction, especially since it can be embarrassing for a man to confront and because it's in such a tender and intimate aspect of the relationship.

MENTAL HEALTH ISSUES

Studies have shown that regularly watching porn can be linked to a range of mental health issues for men, including anxiety, depression, stress and problems with confidence and self-esteem.

ETHICAL DESENSITISATION

The porn industry is, broadly speaking, a really unethical place for women. There are exceptions to this, but they're rare. A lot of research has found widespread exploitation and manipulation of women, physical and psychological damage done to the stars, PTSD and drug addiction. By consuming porn, a person is taking part in that world of false, performative pleasure and genuine exploitation, and there will be moments when they're confronted with this reality. In those moments, they have to make an ethical choice: do I continue to watch pornography where, behind the scenes, a lot of harm is probably being done to these women, or do I choose to stop?

A Pornosexual has probably made the choice that they're fine with women being exploited and hurt just to provide him with excitement. This can have broader implications for his ethics: he may be more likely to neglect, abuse or hurt a woman in real life for his own pleasure.

THE RED FLAGS

- He seems like a different person during sex
- It seems like he's trying to recreate a scenario with you during sex, rather than just enjoying being with you
- When you're not being sexual together, he finds it hard to talk about sex
- He feels cold or distant during sex
- He doesn't seem interested in you as a person, he's just interested in the performance you can provide
- He watches a lot of porn, and sometimes it means he isn't interested or can't perform when you're actually being intimate together

WHAT'S THE UNDERLYING PSYCHOLOGY?

Porn is a multi-billion dollar industry, and the more a man watches, the more money somebody is making. This means that porn creators are hacking a man's brain: they're trying to create as much excitement and arousal as quickly as they can, with as little discomfort and resistance that might make a man switch off. It's the same as sugary foods or nicotine or anything else that causes chemical changes in a man's brain. This means that all porn has the risk of altering a man's biology, his thinking and his emotions.

Over time, as porn has become more mainstream, there's also been a shift in society which panders to the same impulses of arousing men. Breast enlargement and other cosmetic surgeries are more common, people use language about sex more casually than they would have a few decades ago, and most people now accept that men watch a lot of porn, so there's a lot less shame or guilt which might have acted as guardrails for men. I remember one client, who is pretty sexually adventurous and goes on a lot of hookup-style dates, telling me that it's normal now for men to expect anal sex on a first date.

This is patriarchy at work. A whole industry, and shifts in society, designed to please men while ignoring the impacts it might have on genuine sexual connection. Sex is an act of intimacy between two people, while porn is a fake, carefully-crafted performance that's only intended to arouse a man.

Sexual liberation is, of course, a good thing. Sex is there to be enjoyed, and experimenting and learning new ways to experience it is part of personal growth. However, porn is something else. Almost no porn is aimed at women's interests or needs. Porn is generally a carefully created product designed to arouse men and get them off, and this will change the way a man experiences sex.

If he's addicted to porn, a man will need to deal with all of the challenges that come with any addition. These include a lack of self-control, lower self-esteem and confidence, perhaps problems spending too much money and time on his addiction, and all sorts of difficulties maintaining relationships with other people. Some people seem to be more prone to addiction than others, so if a man has tendencies to get addicted to things generally, porn will be no exception. If a man is addicted to porn, he should treat this seriously and get medical or therapeutic support, or at least read books about it and create a plan to address his addiction.

Of course, not all men who are desensitised and altered by porn are addicts. Really we're looking at two important psychological problems: first, is a man addicted to the stimulation he's receiving; second, is his ability to genuinely connect with a sexual partner being affected by the porn he watches? If either of those things are true, he should try to learn more about the effects of porn on his brain, his arousal and his expectations.

At the end of the day, a man needs to have the ability to form genuine, meaningful sexual connections. If he can't be present with this partner during sex, or if he can't get excited unless she is recreating the pornographic experience for him, or if he loses interests in her wants and needs, or if he is too impatient with the pace of real sex because he's used to porn delivering overwhelming stimulation whenever he wants it, or if he isn't able to perform sexually because he's prefering masturbating over porn…then he is being manipulated and negatively impacted by porn.

A man needs the ability to be honest with himself, and he needs to know that he is in control of his impulses, and that he is prioritising real-world connections and sexual experiences over fantasies on his screen. The real danger here is that so many men aren't honest with themselves, and they can fall into the User category of toxic men because they've lost the ability to successfully form real sexual connections.

WHY ARE THESE MEN DANGEROUS?

The main danger of a Pornosexual man is that he'll damage a woman's self-esteem through his unrealistic expectations and inability to connect with her. He might demand things from her that she's uncomfortable with, and leave her with the impression that she's failed as a partner because she won't do the things that porn actresses do. He might have very high expectations for the way she looks, how easily she gets turned on, or how much noise she makes during sex. All of this can leave a woman asking: is there something wrong with me?

A woman might even come to believe that she's *supposed* to do all the things he's demanding, and so she does all sorts of sexual things that don't feel genuine or authentic to her. This can leave her with shame, damaged self-esteem and can make it harder to trust or form connections in the future.

WHAT WOULD HEAL THESE MEN?

If he's not an addict, then a man needs to maintain a good, honest perspective on his relationship with porn. Is it affecting him? Is he losing touch with reality? Are his mental, emotional and physical responses shifting because of porn? A man needs to be really careful to keep answering these questions honestly.

He should also become an expert in the thing he's addicted to. Understand how it's made, what it's doing to his brain, and read books or online accounts from other men about their journeys with porn.

If he has crossed the line into addiction, then a man should seek professional help.

WHY ARE WOMEN ATTRACTED TO THESE MEN?

Most Pornosexuals will hide their porn use, so they'll just seem like regular guys.

Other Pornosexuals wear it proudly: they are openly and obviously sexual, using porn-type language all the time and being suggestive about doing the most outrageous things. This can feel exciting, taboo and stimulating and it can be fun to develop connections with men who are so obviously uninhibited. However, there's a big difference between a man who's sexually confident and adventurous, and a man who's just watched a lot of porn and uses women to recreate what he's seen on the screen. If you're looking for a genuine personal connection with a man, but he turns out to be a Pornosexual, you're going to be disappointed.

Type 7: Poseur

Building new connections with people can be difficult, and we've all developed our own ways to handle it. We learn from people when we're younger, and later in life we might experiment with different ways of connecting with friends or partners. Some people read books about dating, some people get specific coaching about pickup techniques.

Some men are into things that, they discover, make them attractive to women. Musicians or artists, for instance, are famously attractive to certain women. There's something exciting and alluring about a man with the confidence to stand on stage and make music, stirring up emotion in the crowd and showing off his skills. Men who make art can be attractive for other reasons: they're often passionate about subtle, interesting things and they're driven to talk about them. The passion and emotional intensity of artists can be very sexy.

Spiritual men can also stand out as unusual and alluring. Sometimes you will meet a man who is fascinated by the spiritual realm, perhaps a preacher, perhaps someone into meditation and yoga, perhaps men who travel the world sampling different spiritual traditions as they look for the answers their soul is seeking. Some women are intensely attracted to these men. They are often communicative, they possess deep wisdom, and some traditions (like tantra) can focus on strong empathic, sensual connections.

These men are just as complex and varied as any other men, but you will find plenty of toxic men in these spaces too, especially the Poseur. The word, if you're not familiar with it, is used to describe people who craft a false persona, usually a flamboyant one, to get what they want. The word morphed into 'poser', which people use to talk about someone who poses, or puts on an exaggerated persona.

I have spent years of my life in different creative and spiritual circles. I have sat at dawn in a circle of fascinating people, under the open sky, and talked with total vulnerability and candour about things that are really important to me. I've met so many men in those worlds who are good, decent, trustworthy men. Weird, certainly. Creative or spiritual men often break some of the core rules of patriarchal society, so they have to find their own, more authentic rules and they can be complex people. But amongst these men you would always find one or two who felt...slimy. Men whose eyes lingered too long on women. Men who seemed to always turn the conversation to sex. Men who would sit very close to young women and talk about mysterious and exciting things.

These are men who seduce women using (for example) spirituality, music or art. They can also exist in academic circles, or really any area where niche expertise makes men attractive to women. A professor who uses his allure as an older, wiser, powerful man to seduce young students would also be a Poseur.

A Poseur's works to manipulate women who are fascinated by their lifestyle and glamour. The identity the Poseur shows the world is a lie, or a very exaggerated version of himself. He hides behind his mystique, because that seems to be enough to get him into a woman's bed, but he has very limited skills at being genuine or vulnerable with her. He has to maintain the character he's created.

Poseurs, then, are liars who use their unusual persona to seduce women. If they were being honest, they would say they just want sex, but they don't say this. They talk about things from their world. The musician will compose her a song. The yoga teacher will talk to her about prana. The academic will show off his expertise and bamboozle her with his knowledge. It's all an act. It's all about getting her into bed, or winning the affection he craves.

I'm not saying that all men who make art, or music, or devote their lives to spirituality, are this type of toxic man. Poseurs exploit the work of these genuine men. They inhabit the same world, but their motivation is seducing women.

Relationships with these men are usually very unsatisfying, and tend to be brief. All he has is the act, the glamour, the pretence. Behind that, he's an uncommunicative, insecure, manipulative person and he will have to keep up his persona to have any meaningful ongoing connection.

The problem for women is that he works very hard to fool them. Women he doesn't fancy will see through the mask quickly, as will men. Women who trust their intuition will tend to notice how uncomfortable it feels to be around him. This leaves a lot of women who are his targets. He preys on impressionable women, or women who feel a need for things that their current life doesn't offer. Perhaps she craves spiritual fulfilment, or passionate emotions, or more intense sex, or to feel a great sense of wonder at the world. These women won't usually be able to see through his illusions because he's offering them exactly what they're looking for.

THE RED FLAGS

- A flamboyant, intense or eccentric appearance
- The sense that he is 'trying too hard' to seem special or different
- Difficulty or evasiveness when answering questions about things outside of his fake persona, for example about his family, his emotions or his relationship history
- Occasionally being exposed as deeply insecure, upset or afraid
- Fear of leaving behind the accessories of his persona (for example his music, his books or his yoga mat)
- A practised routine to seduce women

WHAT'S THE UNDERLYING PSYCHOLOGY?

Becoming intimately involved with someone is emotionally risky. We spend most of our lives wearing masks and putting up walls to keep ourselves safe, but when we choose to get very close to someone we let them into places that most people never see. Most people naturally develop circles of trust, where most people are kept outside the circle, and only those we trust most are in our circle. Family get a certain level of trust, friends get different levels of trust depending on how safe we feel with them, but ideally our closest relationships should get the highest level of trust. Sure, if you're only expecting a fling with somebody you're not going to open yourself to much emotional risk, but the more we hope to build with someone, the more we open ourselves up to them. It's one of the biggest emotional risks we ever take, because the more we open up and the more we trust somebody, the more capacity they have to hurt us. Their words hit harder, their criticism sting more and if they hurt us, it hurts that much more.

So, we all need to develop skills here. Most people do, as we go through our first few relationships. We learn how to check that this person is worthy of trust, we learn how to open up a bit at a time, we learn how to communicate our needs to somebody even when we're deeply intimate with them, and we learn how to heal after the inevitable bumps and bruises.

The Poseur doesn't learn these skills, he learns other skills instead so he never has to deal with the real risk of being vulnerable and intimate with someone. His skills are about camouflage and masking, about seeming something mysterious and exciting and exotic, but making sure his partner never really gets too close.

There will be reasons why he's never learned to take the ultimate risk and plunge into the complex, wonderful world of deep human intimacy. Perhaps he was hurt badly early in life, and he decided never to risk trusting people again. Perhaps he learned to be dramatic and performative at an early age and immediately realised how quickly he gets people's attention and affection. Perhaps he tried having meaningful relationships but they hurt too much so he switched to being a caricature, projecting a mask to keep himself safe. Perhaps he just never had an opportunity in his developmental years (childhood or teenage life) to practise love and trust, so it's always been a mystery to him.

Whatever his specific reasons, the outcome is the same: he prefers to act a role rather than be an authentic, complex, flawed human being. This role keeps him safe and gets him love, attention, sex, or whatever else he craves. He just doesn't know what to do with women after the initial conquest is over.

WHY ARE THESE MEN DANGEROUS?

Like many men on this list, Poseurs are most dangerous for the psychological damage they do. If a woman is involved with these men, it can be amazing and intoxicating and intense…and then end just as suddenly. She can end up very confused about who to trust, and it can take her years of healing to be willing to let someone get close to her again.

WHAT WOULD HEAL THESE MEN?

Poseurs need to learn to put their seductive personas aside and connect in a truly vulnerable way. This will require learning a lot about healthy ways of relating to women (so books, YouTube or podcasts may help). There's probably some healing work to do as well, to figure out why trust and openness feels so dangerous, and heal these wounds enough to be willing to risk being vulnerable with partners.

WHY ARE WOMEN ATTRACTED TO THESE MEN?

Because Poseurs are sexy! They have crafted a whole identity to seem exciting, or taboo, or mysterious, or liberated. Women who are tired of their boring lives, or who feel trapped and limited by social pressures, or who simply want the attention of an intense man who makes them feel special, will find Poseurs amongst the men they find attractive.

If you are a woman who's reading this and seeing a lot of these kinds of toxic men in your past, I'd encourage you to reflect deeply on your emotional needs. What do these men do for you, that other men don't? Perhaps you need to feel special, perhaps you need freedom from pressures, or perhaps you want to do dramatic things but you need someone else to lead the way. Attraction comes, in large part, when somebody offers to fulfil needs that aren't being met in other ways, or needs that have long been neglected. If you can really clearly identify the needs that are being forgotten in you, you can find safer ways to meet them.

Either way, if you like passionate, eccentric men, be on guard for shallow Poseurs who can't offer you more than the thrill of seduction.

Type 8: Lost boy

We're talking a lot about patriarchal culture in this book: a culture which sets up artificial and unhealthy standards for what a man should be, standards that are impossible to meet without also becoming a toxic and harmful person. It also tells women that their worth is deeply connected to (amongst other things) how much they care for children and for men. Both women and men are capable of internalising patriarchal beliefs, and an internalised belief feels like it's your own idea. But none of us naturally grow into patriarchy: it's something we have to be taught.

Patriarchy warps the childhood of boys and girls in so many ways, but one situation that we've all encountered is the pampered boy and the over-tolerant mother.

We can imagine a young boy growing up in a household where nobody questions patriarchal values. He unconsciously learns that women are there to provide for him. His mother has internalised patriarchy, and so she sees her self-worth as coming from how much she cares for him. She might become smothering and over-protective, but she certainly reinforces his beliefs about the roles of men and women. She may act subservient or pandering, or she may tolerate bad behaviour from him. Our young boy enters adulthood with both an expectation of being cared for, and a dependence on people looking after him.

This is the birth of the Lost Boy type of toxic men. They can be, in other ways, nice people, but they have this unconscious, unquestioned belief that relationships are meant to work in one way: women are meant to look after him. He may or may not be able to voice that belief, it may be lodged well below the conscious level.

Lost Boys move between relationships looking for a mother figure. He'll do what he needs to do to win over this new mother, altering his behaviour in manipulative ways. Some men might try to convince a woman that he's helpless, winning over a partner by triggering her programming to rescue and save men. These relationships become codependent from the first day, and women who fall for this strategy will condemn themselves to a relationship where she's expected to look after his needs at all times.

Other Lost Boys are more subtle about it, they use language that implies his superiority to women, which can feel to a woman like strength and confidence. Again, a woman who enters this relationship will find that actually, she is organising his diary, cooking his meals and ironing his clothes.

Since the Lost Boy believes that the world only makes sense when a woman is looking after him, he's likely to:

- Be dependent on women for his practical needs

- Rely on women to do his emotional processing for him

- Have a sense of superiority towards women, wanting to re-create the situation where women are, effectively, his servants

- Sometimes use infantile language that shows how much he sees his partner as his mother

- Manipulate situations and people so that women need to rescue him or provide for him

- Resent women who don't embody their 'proper' patriarchal roles

- Boss around women at work because, without realising it, he sees all women as his servants

THE RED FLAGS

- Manipulative or coercive behaviour in the early relationship

- Asking or demanding that she look after him: cleaning, tidying or organising his life

- Strong emotional needs and dependence. He might need a lot of reassurance, affection or attention in a way that feels unbalanced to his partner.

- He might need help navigating emotional situations at work or with friends, needing his partner to take the lead or explain situations to him

- He will rarely display leadership or decisiveness

WHAT'S THE UNDERLYING PSYCHOLOGY?

Lost Boys are just men who didn't go through essential steps in their psychological development. Perhaps he never got to experience failure or challenge without someone there to look after him. Perhaps his emotions were constantly smothered by the needs of his parents. Perhaps there were never strong men around to provide examples of leadership, confidence and independence. Whatever went wrong, these men never learned to stand on their own and face all the challenges and problems of an adult life. They unconsciously believe that they need somebody else to handle things for them.

Within developmental psychology we use the term 'individuation' to describe the process of children separating from their parents and becoming their own unique selves. It's essential to become an independent, functioning adult who can handle what life throws at you. This process can get interrupted by all sorts of things, from traumatic experiences to smothering or inconsistent parenting, to being seriously unwell for a period of your childhood.

It is usually possible later in life to develop all the skills that were missed in childhood. Learning fairness of what to expect from friends, family or partners. Emotional resilience in the face of setbacks and conflicts. Self awareness and leadership skills.

Lost Boys are men who haven't done this work, and instead find ways to convince women to look after them.

WHY ARE THESE MEN DANGEROUS?

Unless their demands become physical, the main danger from a Lost Boy is how they might warp a woman's beliefs. A woman in a relationship with a Lost Boy needs to be content being his mother. Parents know that their needs come second to the needs of their children, that's just part of parenting. In adult relationships, both people need to know their needs are equally respected. A Lost Boy will take far more than he gives.

Women in these relationships will need to be ok with their needs not being recognised, respected or satisfied. He won't know or care how to meet you like an adult man. If you're willing to tolerate that, you may find that it'll impact your self-esteem and confidence over time.

WHAT WOULD HEAL THESE MEN?

Lost Boys need to stop believing that it's normal or ok to depend on women for their physical or emotional needs. They need to let go of the idea that their partner should be their mother.

How he does this will depend on the man. If his behaviour comes from his childhood, he'll need to engage in therapy to deeply understand what happened to him, and then grow into a fully mature man.

If it doesn't come from bad lessons, neglect or trauma in his past, and instead he's just let himself be a selfish person who makes all

omeone else's problems, then he just needs to

satisfying, fair and sustainable relationship

...eans a fair balance of needs, which are hon-

.. respected by the other person.

WHY ARE WOMEN ATTRACTED TO THESE MEN?

Some Lost Boys can be very successful in the workplace, because some workplaces feel and operate a lot like dysfunctional families. If his lack of self-awareness, inability to manage his own life and emotional neediness actually works for him at work, he can thrive in business and become quite wealthy. So sometimes women are attracted to Lost Boys simply because they can provide wealth and financial stability.

But in general, women are attracted to Lost Boys because of their own internalised patriarchy. A woman who has internalised the belief that she is *supposed* to care for men, that her role in a relationship is to be caring and nurturing to boys and men, will tend to find Lost Boys attractive. In this case, she needs to dive into feminist books and podcasts to shake off these toxic beliefs and recognise that she is not merely an instrument for meeting a man's needs.

Type 9: Saviour

In my core series of books, the Arete Trilogy, I talk about the Karpman Drama Triangle. This is a psychological model about the masks that we tend to wear throughout our lives and the ways we navigate social experiences at work, at home, in friendships and in love. The three most common masks that people in our culture tend to wear: the Rescuer, the Persecutor and the Victim.

Rescuers are people whose self-esteem is deeply connected to how much they save the people around them. Unless they have rescued or helped someone recently, a Rescuer will feel bad about themselves, because they believe that rescuing others is the thing that gives them value and worth. Both men and women wear the Rescuer mask from time to time, and some people spend big chunks of their lives trapped within this identity.

For some men, this gets bound up with some patriarchal beliefs, like the idea that men are strong and women are weak, and that a man can demonstrate his potency in the world by caring for women. These men believe that their role in life is to save weak women from a difficult world. I'm calling these men Saviours.

The motivations of the Saviour are, like all these toxic male archetypes, mostly unconscious (so he won't understand why he's doing what he's doing). He'll simply feel an unspoken pressure to look after, save, rescue or care for women that he sees as vulnerable.

He will often find himself attracted to women who seem damaged, helpless, struggling or stuck in difficult situations. Even when he isn't pursuing a woman romantically, he will look for ways to save the women in his life. He may have this kind of relationship with his mother, sister or other relatives, and he will be quick to care for women at work.

We aren't talking about a healthy compassion here, which would be aimed at everyone. He has something to gain by rescuing women. He will feel more manly, he'll feel better about himself, he'll feel like the world makes more sense, if he is rescuing a 'poor vulnerable woman'. It's almost predatory.

Men like this in long-term relationships or marriages will run everything, and will regularly try to find new ways to save his partner from some kind of situation. His partner will probably have believed similar things about herself at the start of the relationship (that she is helpless or unable to cope on her own). Even if this wasn't a very strong belief to begin with, she may come to believe this over time. Rather than supporting his partner to develop her own solutions to the challenges life throws at her, and rather than respecting her ability to navigate her life without his help, a Saviour will enjoy her dependence on him. He might sabotage her personal growth, but even if he doesn't, he will tend to point out her mistakes and undermine her ability to thrive. He needs her to be dependent on him.

THE RED FLAGS

- If a woman talks to him about a range of different things, but mentions that she's struggling with something, he will ignore everything else and just talk about the struggle

- He will encourage her to think about how hard things are, reinforcing the idea that she can't handle life on her own

- He's quick to offer suggestions, solutions or help when women are facing difficulties

- He rushes to rescue women when he notices them struggling

- Others might find him 'smothering' to be around

WHAT'S THE UNDERLYING PSYCHOLOGY?

The Saviour's identity grows out of two things: his fragile self-esteem and his patriarchal beliefs about the roles of women and men in society.

One of the ways you can tell someone's level of self-esteem is by watching how much they depend on external validation. Do they respond really strongly to positive and negative feedback? Do they ask for reassurance a lot? Are they trying to prove to themselves or others that they're a good person by showing off their success, their wealth, their clever ideas, their looks or their role in a community? People with low self-esteem are often looking for things outside of themselves to reassure them that they're a good person, that they're strong, that they're worthy of love etc.

That's exactly what the Saviour is doing. For some reason, his self-esteem is quite fragile. He might feel good about himself sometimes, but it doesn't take much for him to question his worth. For example, money troubles, or being reprimanded at work, or a fight with his partner, or just having a bad day. He'll start to feel crap about himself, doubting himself and looking for reassurance or something to soothe his emotions.

A Saviour has also internalised the patriarchal belief that women are weaker than men, or that men have a duty to protect and rescue women from harm. This might seem noble in some scenarios, but you have to believe that you're stronger or better than something in order to believe that you can protect or rescue it. These kinds of beliefs infantilize women (that is, it treats women like infants or little children).

He might know that he believes this, and he might be quite comfortable with the idea that women are weaker, more emotional, less resilient or less intelligent than him. These men will be casually patronising and demeaning to women. Thankfully these men are less common now, as misogyny is less acceptable in most places, which means that Saviours are more likely to have complex, hidden motives.

Most Saviours today would say that they respect women, that they are an ally to women, but somewhere deep in their minds is the idea that women are just a little bit feeble, and that he should be rescuing and protecting them. He's not disrespecting them, just for standing up for them, right? And yet, we see a consistent pattern of rescuing from him, of him acting like women need him, and we see him encouraging women to focus on how overwhelmed and vulnerable they feel.

This is very different to being a genuine ally of women, which means challenging patriarchal behaviour or structures and then getting out of the way to let a woman handle her own problems, in the full respect that she's just as capable as any man.

WHY ARE THESE MEN DANGEROUS?

Saviours are really good at amplifying internalised patriarchy in women. If a woman has some beliefs (whether it be conscious or deeply buried) that she is vulnerable, weak or unable to cope, simply because she's a woman, then a Saviour will prey on this belief. His actions, over time, will make it more intense and if he's allowed to, he will make it literally true by making a woman dependent on him. To him, this will feel right and proper, and he will feel like a good man for helping her so much. But for a woman in a relationship with him, this will feel like her independence and confidence is being washed away.

A successful, healthy relationship is where there's genuine mutual respect. Even if she becomes a stay-at-home parent, he can respect the hard work she's doing every day to raise the kids. As we discussed earlier in this book, a great relationship feels like teamwork.

Two people, with deep respect for one another, solving life's problems together.

This isn't what it feels like to be in a relationship with a Saviour. It can feel really nice in the short term to have your needs met, to be saved from challenges, or to have your responsibilities taken care of. However, if there's a demeaning patriarchal belief behind it all, it will begin to feel smothering, or disrespectful, or belittling. A woman in a relationship like this will usually, over time, come to believe that she can't cope without him, that she is in fact weak, that she needs his opinions about things, or that he's the leader in the relationship. This will come with a steady lowering of her self-esteem, self-belief and confidence.

WHAT WOULD HEAL THESE MEN?

Saviours who are conscious about their beliefs and obvious in the way they act are very close to being Misogynists, so they'll be healed by the same things as Type 1.

Saviours who have more complex beliefs and motives need to be challenged about what's really going on inside them. These men tell everyone, including themselves, that they're a good guy and that they respect women, but they continue to jump at every change to rescue any woman they think needs them. Do these men really see women as equals? Do they need to explore their beliefs more deeply?

These men benefit a lot from the example of healthy male role models. Once they see how other men, who have done the work to root out their patriarchal programming, handle situations at work or in relationships, they will (hopefully) begin to realise how weird their behaviour is.

WHY ARE WOMEN ATTRACTED TO THESE MEN?

It's really nice to have someone do nice things for you. It's nice to be noticed when you're struggling and helped. It's nice to know that somebody cares. Sometimes it's nice to have somebody step in and take away your burdens for a while. Everyone struggles with things, and for a while it can be such a relief to not have to struggle.

However, patriarchy is so cunning at worming its way into our minds. We're drip-fed patriarchal ideas all the time by advertising, songs, movies and by people we meet. It's there inside almost all of us, waiting to be activated. So it's very easy to go from appreciating someone's help, to beginning to be dependent on them, to eventually believing you can't cope without them.

Type 10: Sleepwalker

This type of toxic man is so common that many women have just come to accept that this is how men are. This is the man who likes regular routines, who comes home from work and puts his feet up to watch TV. He doesn't like things changing, he doesn't like to be disturbed. He grows more distant from his friends and he stops making an effort to go out and socialise. He sees it all as too much hassle. His comfort zone is very small: he has a few friends, he stays at home a lot, he might go on holiday to the same places he's been before, he's very set in his ways, with strong opinions that never seem to change. In a relationship, he will often feel he's being 'nagged' a lot but a dissatisfied partner. She is the one who drags him to events, she's the one who dreams of doing new things or trying new hobbies together, she wishes he would take her out to a restaurant or buy her flowers or just do *something* that isn't his safe little comfort zone.

These men are the Sleepwalkers: never very awake, never very high or very low, they just plod through life doing predictable things all the time.

How is this toxic? Being a Sleepwalker doesn't mean he's violent or mean or manipulative or hurtful. His only addiction is to comfort and familiarity. So long as his partner is happy to live this kind of life, there's no massive problem, right?

But I have to ask: what is the point of being alive? If you think the point of being alive is to live a safe, comfortable, predictable life then a Sleepwalker is a great partner. However, I think the point of being alive is to experience things, to be truly conscious and present, to form deep and meaningful connections with people, to have a sense of purpose and commitment in your life, to regularly challenge yourself to step out of your comfort zone and face fears and do completely new things. To live with passion and presence and purpose. I believe every human being yearns to feel these things, once their basic needs have been met. I've written a whole trilogy of books about how you achieve a life like this.

So the danger of a Sleepwalker is the years that slide by, unmarked and unremarkable, while he continues to plod through his predictable and safe life. His partner learning to accept that this is the best she can hope for. People often look back on these times with regret for all the things they could have done with that time.

And while there are, of course, loads of women out there who fall into the same trap, it does seem to be much more common in men. We all know couples where the woman still seems to be dynamic, expressive, curious and engaged while the man is switched-off, boring and passive. So many characters in books, TV shows and movies follow this trope. Because it's real, and in my opinion it's a huge loss for both the men themselves and for their partners and friends.

THE RED FLAGS

- He would always rather stay at home than go out

- He wants to do the same things all the time, with the same people

- He comes up with reasons to avoid doing anything new, and over time he might shape his beliefs about the world so that he can stay in his comfort zone

- He feels like life is already hard, so why make it any harder by doing unfamiliar things?

- Sometimes his fear (of failure, of the unknown, of challenging himself) breaks through his veneer of indifference

WHAT'S THE UNDERLYING PSYCHOLOGY?

The Sleepwalker identity is built upon two foundation stones. The first is the tendency of human beings in this culture to tend towards safety and familiarity. So much of our society is based around the idea of comfort and security. There is a neurological habit in all mammals to want to do things that feel safe, and to stick with them, but in pre-modern times this was balanced by all the daily risks and adversity we faced in the natural world. Today, this brain habit runs out of control. Unless we challenge ourselves regularly, we settle into comfort zones and we begin to diminish as people. Our drive, our confidence and our ability to handle challenges all shrink and we begin to become more and more scared of the things outside the comfort zone.

This affects everyone, it's just a thing our brains do and it's made much worse by the culture we live in.

For men, there is another challenge that accelerates this collapse into mediocrity: the crisis in modern masculinity. Men don't know what they're supposed to be. They're bombarded with conflicting messages about what a successful man looks like. Is Donald Trump the ideal man, with his wealth, his debauchery and his overwhelming self-confidence? Is the ideal man someone who's humble and never bothers anyone, but who doesn't believe in himself much? Should a man be sleeping with hundreds of women to prove himself? Should he live by a moral code or should he do whatever it takes to win? Should he sculpt a perfect physique and appearance, or is that vain and weird?

Women have similar challenges, but they have actively engaged with the questions. When a woman wants to figure out what it means to be a successful woman, there are plenty of books and resources, and while they can be conflicting and put huge pressure on women to perform, there is at least a consistent message in modern feminism: believe in yourself, for who you are. Many men haven't found this truth for themselves, they're still looking for a template to follow, and when something tells them that they've failed as a man, it often hurts them deeply.

For many men, it's better not to engage with the questions at all. They already have all of the challenges of adulthood to deal with, adding deep personal and philosophical questions on top of them just feels overwhelming. So they settle into their comfort zones and they just try to get through each day. The messaging from this culture of security and predictability works very well for them.

WHY ARE THESE MEN DANGEROUS?

Sleepwalkers are dangerous because life is short, and how we spend our days is important. A sleepwalker will encourage his partner to also stay in her comfort zone. He will amplify the voices that say: stay in that boring job, keep meeting up with the same boring friends, don't do anything reckless or new, don't challenge yourself to grow, save for your pension and die quietly.

You cannot grow as a person *and* be comfortable. All growth comes from challenge, from trying new things, from facing fears and going beyond what feels safe. If you want to feel alive, to be present in each moment, if you want to feel confident and strong in yourself, if you want to look back on your life when you're older with pride and satisfaction, then you need to grow as a person, all the time. We all need to commit to challenging ourselves regularly, in order to maintain a healthy mind.

If a man is deeply committed to his comfort zone then he will be very uncomfortable being uncomfortable. That will make him hostile to new ideas, to disruption, to being challenged…and that means he's hostile to living a passionate, happy life.

WHAT WOULD HEAL THESE MEN?

Sleepwalkers need to heal their addiction to the comfort zone, and also find their own way to feel good as a man while being bombarded with conflicting messages about manhood.

My core trilogy of books, called the Arete Trilogy, is designed to help people move beyond the comfort zone. We have to learn that facing risk and challenge is good for us, and learn to embrace the discomfort, knowing it makes a more capable, stronger, more confident person.

In terms of finding his own way in his masculinity, that means learning as much as possible. He needs to find out what men are saying about it. He needs to dig deeply into his core beliefs and motives, ideally with a professional like a coach or therapist who can ask him helpful questions. He needs to make up his own mind about what he stands for and what success means for him.

WHY ARE WOMEN ATTRACTED TO THESE MEN?

Sleepwalkers can be lovely men. They can be caring, supportive, fun (in a limited sort of way), and they feel safe and comfortable to be around. Women often meet them before they become Sleepwalkers, and then have to watch as their partner slowly becomes more and more boring. Other women are looking for a Sleepwalker because they too fear leaving the comfort zone and they want a partner who will provide a safe, predictable home.

How to stop being attracted to toxic men

WORK ON YOUR BOUNDARIES AND SELF-ESTEEM

Decide what you're willing to tolerate, and don't settle for anything less. Keep your standards high. Just because there are a lot of Misogynists, Users and Stones out there, don't sacrifice your own self-respect just to have a partner.

It's essential for all of us to understand our core motivating values, and to have a clear picture of the life we want to build for ourselves. When you're thinking about the kind of partner you want, aim high. Don't let your experience of crappy partners bring your standards down. Expect a lot from your partner and, when you're in a relationship, be sure to keep checking that he's still measuring up. So many men morph into Sleepwalkers when they're settled in relationships.

If you know that your self-esteem is a bit low, commit to working on that whether or not you're in a relationship. Work on it as a gift to yourself. Read books, find inspiring podcasts and engage in therapy work.

The ideal relationship is one where both people encourage each other to be their best selves. This doesn't look like nagging or pressure, but rather just holding ourselves and our partners to high standards and trying to meet them in the way we live our lives.

UNDERSTAND WHY YOU'RE ATTRACTED TO TOXICITY

Sexual attraction is complicated, but it begins with how you respond emotionally and mentally to the way somebody behaves. Maybe it's old memories or conditioning being triggered, maybe it's a tone of voice or the way someone stands, it can even be a smell. These are the first triggers that tell your brain: yes, this person is attractive, go for this guy.

If you keep finding that you're excited by things that don't meet your standards, that's a thing to examine carefully. Start journaling about what's happening inside you when you're around these kinds of men. Find ways to learn about what's going on. Perhaps hire a therapist who can ask helpful questions about why you respond to toxic men like this.

TEACH YOURSELF THAT HEALTHY IS ATTRACTIVE

Start wondering about the kinds of men you do want to be with. If you find that your mind is willing to consider these men but your feelings and your body don't get excited, don't despair! That's ok as a place to start. The things you're attracted to can shift over time, as you spend time with healthier men and as you do the healing work to understand how patriarchy has conditioned you. A healed person finds respect, equality and deep emotional connection attractive, so just keep walking down this path until you begin to

Asking men the right questions

Here are some good questions to ask men when you're getting close to them:

- How do you see your future?
- Tell me about women you've respected and why?
- Have you ever been to therapy?
- What did you learn about yourself through therapy?
- What's your love language?
- What motivates you to pursue your goals?
- What scares you about the way men behave?
- Other than physical, what are the most attractive qualities in a woman?
- What are you working to improve about yourself?

A final word: Commitment to ongoing growth

I hope you've found this book helpful and insightful, and I hope it helps you build more fulfilling, happier, safer relationships.

As a parting comment, I just want to remind you that personal growth never stops. I've talked a lot about patriarchal programming in this book, because it's toxic and it's something we're all exposed to. It takes so much work to understand how you've been influenced by patriarchy, and to dig out the last tendrils of its influence in your thinking and feeling.

The first main goal of personal development is learning control. We all need to be sure that *we* are the ones making our choices: not our parents, not the memories of a teacher or bully at school, not our fears and not unconscious aspects of our personalities. We need to be sure that we understand our choices and we feel empowered and free to choose whatever life will make us happy.

Rooting out childhood programming is just one part of this. So I invite you to commit to a life of ongoing growth, healing, coming home to your true self and becoming the most badass version of yourself possible.

RECOMMENDED BOOKS

Attachment Theory
A Guide to Strengthening the Relationships in Your Life
by Thais Gibson (2020)

Daring Greatly
How the Courage to Be Vulnerable Transforms the Way We Live,
Love, Parent, and Lead
by Brené Brown (2015)

Fix the System, Not the Women
by Laura Bates (2023)

How to Be an Adult
A Handbook on Psychological and Spiritual Integration
by David Richo (1991)

King Warrior Magician Lover
Rediscovering the Archetypes of the Mature Masculine
by Robert Moore and Douglas Gillette (1992)

Nonviolent Communication
A Language of Life
by Marshall B. Rosenberg (2003, repub 2015)

Self-Parenting
The Complete Guide to Your Inner Conversations
by John K Pollard and Linda Nusbaum (1987, repub 2018)

The Language of Emotions
What Your Feelings are Trying to Tell You
by Karla McLaren (2010)

The Wild Edge of Sorrow
Rituals of Renewal and the Sacred Work of Grief
by Francis Weller (2015)

OTHER BOOKS
FROM THE AUTHOR

Printed in Great Britain
by Amazon

45188471R00126